John Freeman

FAMOUS COUPLES OF THE BIBLE

Brian L. Harbour

BROADMAN PRESS
Nashville, Tennessee

Dedicated to
my wife
Jan
who has enabled me to become a couple
my strongest supporter
my most helpful critic
my best friend
and
the love of my life

4283-14

Dewey Decimal Classification: 220.92
Subject heading: BIBLE-BIOGRAPHY
Library of Congress Catalog Card Number: 78-60053
Printed in the United States of America

Preface

A shattering experience occurred when we received our new church directories. The pictures in the directory had been taken six months before the final publication arrived at the church. On the first page there were pictured a husband and wife who were no longer living together. A few pages later I spotted another such couple. So I began to count them. To my dismay I discovered seven couples, active in our church, who had separated or divorced since the pictures were made. At that moment, the harsh reality of the instability of the family was brought home to me.

The institution of marriage is being strained to its limits in our day. The old adage, "there's no place like home," is not always true. Rather than being a haven of rest, the home is becoming a hell on earth for more and more individuals.

Divorce is becoming increasingly more common. One out of every three couples who begin marriage with stars in their eyes will find the excitement and expectation of today transformed into the bitterness and hostility of tomorrow. Marriage vows are exchanged for marriage blues. Relationships which are meant to endure "till death do us part" are aborted prematurely.

In addition, there is what might be called psychological divorce. That is, all homes that are dead are not marked with the official tombstone of a legal divorce. There are many couples who continue to live together but with minimal communication. The relationship is shattered. The love is gone. The stars have all been hidden behind the clouds, and for all practical purposes the marriage is dead. Dr. James A. Peterson, a foremost authority on marriage and family life, reports on an extensive study of couples who had been married between twenty and twenty-five years. The conclusion? Only six couples out of every hundred were satisfied and fulfilled by their marriage relationship.[1] Many couples are still physically intact, but the psychological oneness no longer exists.

These are facts which indicate a serious problem! There was more truth than facetiousness when a certain justice of the peace put up a sign saying, "Gone to lunch. Be back in an hour. Think it over." We had better face the fact that this is a time of instability in the family.

Much of the pressure on the family comes from the outside, from the false philosophies and luring temptations of the world. The greatest crisis facing the home, though, is not bombardment from without but deterioration from within. Instead of becoming one flesh, bound together by an ever-expanding and deepening love, many couples find themselves pushed apart by their inability to get along.

We need help from every possible source. To the Christian, our basic source is the Bible. Not just the principles proposed but also the personal experiences described in the Scriptures provide some keen insights into the dynamics of marriage. My hope is that these discussions on some of the famous couples of the Bible will provide help for strengthening your marriage.

A special word of thanks goes to my wife, Jan, whose encouragement has kept me at the task and whose willingness to let me use the late night hours for writing has enabled me to finish the project.

I also want to say a word of appreciation to the people at Shiloh Terrace Baptist Church in Dallas who listened to most of this material in sermon form and whose positive response encouraged me to put the material in writing.

Contents

1

Where Did They Go Wrong?

Adam and Eve
Genesis 2:18 to 3:20

It all started with Adam and Eve. They were the first couple, and there were certainly some privileges which accompanied that distinction. There was no one around to complain, "I don't know what the younger generation is coming to." There were no in-law problems. Adam did not have to listen to Eve describe all of the other men she could have married. Nor did Eve have to endure Adam's comparison of her cooking to the way his mother cooked. It was a brand-new experiment.

The Bible describes this new experiment in these words: "And the Lord God said, 'It isn't good for man to be alone; I will make a companion for him, a helper suited to his needs.' Then the Lord God caused the man to fall into a deep sleep, and took one of his ribs and closed up the place from which he had removed it, and made the rib into a woman, and brought her unto the man. 'This is it!' Adam exclaimed. 'She is part of my own bone and flesh! Her name is "woman" because she was taken out of a man.' This explains why a man leaves his father and mother and is joined to his wife, in such a way that the two become one person" (Gen. 2:18, 21-24, TLB).

Perhaps you women would like the slightly altered rendition of that story by a little girl. When asked to describe the creation of man, she said, "God reached down his hands, picked up some modeling clay, and made a man.

When he looked at man, he said, 'I think I can do better than that if I tried again.' So then he created woman!"

Why did God use a rib with which to make woman? According to Jewish tradition, God made woman not from man's head to lord over him, nor from his feet to be trampled under by him, but from his side to be equal to him, from under his arm to be protected by him, from near his heart to be loved by him.

It seemed like a pretty good plan as the relationship was initiated in Genesis 2. Do not overlook the fact that Adam and Eve were brought together under the leadership of God to fulfill his plan for companionship between a man and woman. This was the first attempt by man to experience the fullness of marital bliss, and what a beginning they had. Imagine having God himself to perform your wedding ceremony! Adam and Eve were meant to be happy together, to truly become one flesh. However, a quick glance at Genesis 3 indicates that things did not turn out as planned.

Where did this first couple go wrong? What deprived them of the joys of marital bliss?

They Left God Out

God placed Adam and Eve in a beautiful garden, provided ample food to eat, presented them with a responsibility to occupy their time and gave them a purpose for which to live. God also placed a limitation on their lives. "From any tree of the garden you may eat freely," God said, "but from the tree of the knowledge of good and evil you shall not eat" (Gen. 2:16-17).

Why the limitation? It was not that God wanted to deprive Adam and Eve of something. Nor did he intend to set a trap into which man would inevitably fall. Why, then, did God not want man to eat the fruit of that special tree? God was trying to protect man. He knew man was not able to handle the responsibility that eating the fruit would incur. So God said, "Abundant life in your marriage begins with obedience to my will. Trust me, obey me, and you will be happy." But Genesis 3 shows Adam and Eve's refusal to trust God and to obey him. God was removed from the central place in their marriage for they chose to leave him out of their decision-making process.

How modern Adam and Eve were. The greatest single cause of difficulty in the home today is a lack of spiritual concern. Either purposely or inadvertently, we leave God out of our marriage. But marriage was not meant to be a duet. It was meant to be a holy trio between a man and a woman who love each other and the God whom they serve. This is the way God set it up. This is the way he planned it. As the psalmist said, "Unless the Lord builds the house,/They labor in vain who build it" (127:1). A deliberate decision to put God in charge of our marriages would provide the salve which would heal many wounds.

As old-fashioned as that may seem to some, the presence of God does make a difference in the home. In the family where both the husband and wife are Christians, where they read the Bible together daily and pray together, where they attend church together—that is in homes where God is real—there is a uniting force which is absent in marriages where God is ignored.

Sometimes it is not a question of whether your family is in church, but whether Jesus Christ is in your family. Does Jesus live in your home? Do you allow him to rule? A new pastor visited his members for the purpose of getting acquainted. At one home the husband was out, so the minister visited with the wife. Later that night the woman reported the visit to her husband. "The pastor asked a disturbing question," she told her husband. "He asked me if Jesus lived in our home." The head of the house, quite indignant, retorted, "Didn't you tell him that we are the most substantial givers in the church? Didn't you tell him we are charter members? Didn't you tell him that we are there every time the doors are open?" "No," she returned, "that's not what he asked. He asked if Jesus lived in our home." That's the key question.

A preacher visited an old feudal castle in England. The castle was so old that one of its towers dated back to the fifteenth century. At breakfast the minister noticed high overhead a massive beam that spanned the grand, old hall and bore the following inscription: "That house shall be preserved and never shall decay, where Almighty God is worshipped day by day."

What a testimony concerning the home! When you pray together as a family, are active in a church together, serve God together, and make God the determining factor in every decision, you are establishing a solid foundation for your home. But when you leave God out of your marriage, you are headed for trouble. That's what happened to Adam and Eve.

They Lost Something Special

The honeymoon was quickly over for Adam and Eve, and they lost their first love. That precious closeness of the first days somehow slipped away. Look at Genesis 2:25. The Bible says, "And the man and his wife were both naked and were not ashamed." Each saw the other as he was, with no masks, no facade and neither was embarrassed or ashamed. But then look at Genesis 3:6-7. "When the woman saw that the tree was good for food and that it was a delight to the eyes, and that the tree was desirable to make one wise, she took from its fruit and ate; and she gave also to her husband with

14

her, and he ate. Then the eyes of both of them were opened, and they knew that they were naked; and they sewed fig leaves together and made themselves loin coverings." In that moment, Adam and Eve realized that they had lost something. The spark, the special closeness, the zest was no longer there.

It is frightening how often this same realization comes to the surface in marriages today. Dr. Joyce Brothers receives an average of five thousand calls a day during her program on the radio. She said that the callers repeatedly ask the same basic question: "How can I restore zest to my life and marriage?" [1]

One little boy may be smarter than his teacher thought. She told her class that the system of marriage in which a man had several wives was called polygamy. When she asked what the system of marriage was called in which one man had one wife, the little boy answered, "Monotony." How often we lose something precious in our marriage.

Sometimes it is because of a lack of common courtesy. Before the marriage the lover runs around to the other side of the car to open the door for his beloved. After the marriage it is, "What's the matter? Is your arm broken?"

We recently went out to eat with a couple. As we were seated, the husband graciously held the chair for his wife. She told him, "What are you trying to prove? That's the first time you've done that in five years!" How long has it been since you opened the car door for your wife? Or helped her be seated at a table? Or sent her candy? Or gave her flowers? How often we neglect the common courtesies. The romance comes to a screeching halt. The marriage catches a bad case of the blahs. Something precious has been lost.

15

Sometimes it is because we change. One comedian described the process like this, "Remember fellows when you were just going steady with a girl. You couldn't do anything wrong. At first she would tell you, 'Don't ever change. I love you just the way you are.' So you get married and right away she goes to work on you. She changes the way you dress, the way you eat, makes you live in a different place, have different friends. Then five years later she comes to you and says, 'I don't know. You've changed. You're not the same man I married.' "

Sometimes it is because we become preoccupied in our own activities, in our own work. Selfishness is one of the main sources of problems in the home. Somehow when we walk down the aisle it causes an alteration of our value system. One girl told her mother, "John spends so much money on me. I wish I could think of some way to get him to quit spending so much." Her mother said, "Marry him." That does seem to alter things.

Sometimes it is because we no longer communicate. Ann Landers declares, "If my mail is a fair reflection of what goes on with Mr. and Mrs. America behind closed doors (and I think it is), most marital problems stem from the inability of two people to talk to each other." [2] We will devote an entire chapter to this problem.

I married a young couple recently. You should have seen the stars in their eyes. They were experiencing all the joy and excitement of the beginning of marriage. It brought to mind the excitement with which I approached marriage. But regardless of the excitement with which you begin marriage, if you allow these common failures to occur—when you forget to be courteous, when you change and forget to tell each other, when you think more of yourself than of your mate, when you fail to communicate—then you are headed for trouble because that's what happened to Adam and Eve.

16

They Looked to Greener Pastures

Notice something else in this story. Eve looked to greener pastures. Just think of what she had. Eve had a garden paradise in which to live. She had a husband who loved her. She had a marriage which was formed in the very mind of God. She had the fruit from all the trees in the garden (except one) to be her food. She was under God's protection. She had everything she needed. Yet, instead of seeing what she had, she began to look at what she did not have. The more she looked, the more she liked. Finally, she fell victim to that myth which has repeatedly reaped its destruction in the world, the myth that the grass is greener on the other side of the fence.

We see this myth luring man in every area of life. The other person's life always seems easier, his problems seem less serious, his house looks prettier, his children easier to manage, his job more exciting, his church more challenging, his grass greener than ours, and other marriages appear to be more fulfilling. This is the reason for the restlessness of so many men and women. This is the reason for the increased infidelity of our day. Instead of dealing positively with the problem in our own home, we begin to look elsewhere. The other person's husband or wife seems to be more exciting, more attractive, more enjoyable than our own.

I once saw a cartoon which showed a rooster strutting around with all of his chickens. On the other side of the fence were some more chickens. Some boys were playing football on the other side of the fence and accidently threw the ball over into the chicken yard. The rooster looked at the football, looked at his hens, looked at the chickens on the other side of the fence, and said, "I don't mean to gripe, girls, but I wish you would look at the size of the eggs they're putting out on that side!" So it is in the home—the grass always seems greener on the other side.

Consider the case of a woman named Gina. Her husband, George, would come home at night, eat his dinner, then fall asleep in front of the television. He never talked. He never did anything exciting. On a scale of one to ten, their sex life would rate about minus three. So Gina decided to compensate by having an affair with a man named Fred. Fred was about her husband's age but seemed so different. He would talk to her after dinner. He paid attention to her opinions. He showed his affection in obvious ways. She was seriously considering a divorce from George which would free her to marry Fred. Then one day at the beauty parlor she met Peg, Fred's wife. In their conversation, Peg complained about her husband. He did not pay any attention to her. He hardly talked to her when he came home. He had lost all interest in sex. Quite frankly, she said, he was boring. You see, when it came to his own wife, glamor-boy Fred was just as stodgy as George. Gina discovered the truth that always eventually dawns on us: the grass is not greener on the other side. The same problems will crop up. The solution is not to reach out for the supposedly greener grass of your neighbors, but to cultivate the grass in your own yard.

They Located the Blame Elsewhere

There is yet one more important idea in this story of the first couple. Adam and Eve refused to accept any responsibility for what had happened to them. God said, "What happened? Why have you disobeyed? Why is the marriage falling apart?" What did they say? Adam said, "The woman whom Thou gavest to be with me, she gave me from the tree, and I ate" (3:12).

"It was her fault," Adam charged.

"Then the Lord God said to the woman, 'What is this

you have done?' And the woman said, 'The serpent deceived me, and I ate' " (v. 13).

"It was the snake's fault," Eve charged. No one wanted to accept the blame. But it was Eve's fault. Although the temptation was there, she did not have to yield to it. She was to blame. And it was Adam's fault, too. He did not have to eat the fruit. Neither was willing to assume the responsibility for the problem. Neither was willing to say, "It was my fault." Neither was willing to be the initiator in reconciliation by saying, "I'm sorry."

There was a lot of wisdom in what one old man said. He and his wife were country people who lived on the farm all their lives. When they reached their fiftieth year together, the wife was so happy that she wanted to celebrate. She told her husband, "Fifty years ago we got married, Jeb. Let's kill a pig." He answered, "Ma, there ain't no sense in murdering a pig for something we did fifty years ago."

Why blame the problems in our marriage on our business, or on the pressures against us, or on our environment, or on our improper beginning as husband and wife, or on our children—why murder the pig for something we have done!

One of the biggest lies propagated in our day came out of the movie, *Love Story*. It was a powerful movie which produced this dramatic one-liner, "Love means never having to say you're sorry." That's just not true. Love—real love—means facing the reality of your failure, accepting your part of the responsibility, and being willing to say, "I'm sorry." It means to be willing to locate the blame where it belongs many times, on yourself.

Conclusion

I do not know where you are in your marriage. I do not know what problems plague your marriage. But several facts seem certain.

1. If something is wrong in your marriage, then you are to blame—at least partly. It is possible for one person to destroy a marriage, but usually the guilt is shared.

2. Regardless of what has happened, God will help you put it together again. The Bible proclaims our heavenly Father to be the God of the impossible. The word *impossible* appears in the New Testament in reference to God only nine times. Five of those times the word is used to teach that nothing is impossible with God. There are no hopeless cases when God is called in.

3. Someone has to take the initiative. Usually, it is the woman who first seeks help. Cecil Osborne concluded that in seven out of eight instances, women are first to seek help.[3] The important point is that someone must take the initiative. Someone has to have enough courage to admit a need and seek help for it.

4. Both partners have to want improvement. God intended marriage to be a relationship to which two people contributed. Both partners must be willing to recommit themselves to the task.

At the "Little Brown Church" near Nashua, Iowa, the pastor has a unique way of communicating this truth. After the ceremony he walks with the couple to the entrance of the church and says, "Before you go, the bride has the honor of ringing the bell." However, the bell is so heavy that she cannot ring it by herself. The minister says to the groom, "Lend a hand." Together they pull and the bell rings. Then the minister says to the couple, "Never forget that as long as you pull together you can ring the bell." [4]

Pull together, and you can make the bells begin ringing in your marriage once more.

2

The Twenty-Year Itch

Abraham and Sarah
Genesis 16:1-6

A man sat with his wife in the office of a family counselor. It was their first visit and the woman had evidently been the one who insisted on the session. The counselor asked her what the problem was. She responded with a barrage of complaints against her husband. Then the counselor addressed the man, "What do you think is wrong?" The man responded, "Old what's-her-name says I don't love her anymore." Say what you will about that marriage, this much is clear—the honeymoon was over.

Another lady applied for a divorce after sixty years of marriage. When the judge asked her why she wanted a divorce after being married for so long, she answered, "Because enough is enough."

Another woman advertised in a newspaper for a husband. She received scores of replies. The replies were all from other women who said, "You can take mine!"

The commonality that ties these three experiences together is the fact that sometimes marriages, begun in the heat of passion, are cooled off by the passing of time. A marriage, like the individuals in marriage, goes through stages.

The *postnatal* stage in a marriage usually covers the first year. The honeymoon attitude still prevails. Years two to five might be labeled *infancy,* as a balance is developed between freedom and limitations. The *adolescent* stage of marriage begins after about five years, a time when an identity crisis is usually experienced. The *young adulthood* stage lasts until about the fifteenth year. The *middle years* stage comes from fifteen to twenty-five years of marriage. Then the final stage is the stage of *maturity*.

It is becoming increasingly more evident that one of the periods of greatest tension is that of the middle years of marriage. Bernard Harnik suggests that during this period a marriage will go through a second maturing crisis which can finally destroy or further develop the marriage.[1]

A recent study of marriage in the middle years summarized the mood of the relationship at this point as that of "disenchantment." In this study it was revealed that only 6 percent of the wives were very satisfied with their marriages after twenty-two years of living with their husbands. In most cases, it was not just a matter of dissatisfaction but of actual disengagement. The years had gradually pushed the mates apart. They did not talk as much. They did not share as much. They did not laugh as much. They did not love as much. The twenty-year itch had set in.[2]

It is not clear how long Abraham and Sarah were married at the time of the incident in Genesis 16, but they were evidently in the middle years of their marriage. Abraham was eighty-six. Sarah, ten years younger (17:17), was seventy-six. In the life span of their day, this could be considered middle age. This was not a marriage in the early years when the honeymoon attitude still prevailed and the excitement of developing a new relationship still existed. Instead, it was a marriage in the middle years when the twenty-year itch had already begun to settle in. The relationship of Abraham and Sarah can therefore provide some keen insights into the problems of and prescriptions for marriage during the twenty-year crisis in our day.

22

The Problems

When a man and woman have been married for fifteen to twenty years, they will fall into that age group called "middle age." Both their physical age and the age of their marriage will present unique problems which will challenge their relationship. All of these are reflected or implied in the relationship of Abraham and Sarah.

For one thing, there will be *physical problems.* Look at the text. Genesis 16:2; 17:17; 18:11; and 18:12 all indicate that the physical problems which are an inescapable part of growing older were already being experienced by Abraham and Sarah. Sarah was past the age of child bearing (16:2). Abraham, too, felt that he was beyond the age when he could father a child (17:17). They were "stricken with age" (18:11, KJV) which indicates the physical frailties that accompany aging. "It ceased to be with Sarah after the manner of women" (18:11, KJV). That is, she had passed through menopause.

These physical problems are a very real part of the twenty-year itch today. For instance, experts today say that both men and women go through a "change of life" experience during this period which causes hormone and circulatory difficulties which often lead to anxiety. Although Cecil Osborne suggests that male menopause is emotional instead of physiological, some indicate there are physiological bases for the emotional change.[3] Like all anxieties, the anxiety of menopause is the source of multitudes of unreasonable and unpredictable reactions. Explosive outbursts followed by days of deep depression shattered by further outbursts are typical of this time. And lots of tears. Many homes during the middle years are run by water power.

Another part of the physical change is a loss of energy. As we get older, our energy level lowers and we simply cannot do as much. Someone has defined this middle-age period as the time when "feeling your best is not feeling as good as you used to when you were feeling no better than you should." Another has said that middle age is when you feel like the morning after the night before. This is probably why people say that youth looks forward, old age looks backward, and middle age looks worried! Physically, we are not able to do as much. Because we so often measure the worth of a man by his activity, this drop in energy level is a threatening experience for both men and women.

When we move from the romantic to the rheumatic stage of life, when the twenty-year itch sets in, physical problems arise which can destroy your marriage if they are not understood.

There are also *relational problems*. These, too, are clearly revealed in our text. The relationship of Abraham and Sarah was strained by the entrance of another woman. The fact that Sarah suggested the arrangement did not erase the bitterness and hostility that she felt because of it. The effect of children on marriage in the middle years is reflected in our text, although in a different way. It was not the children who were there, but the child who was not there which caused the tension in the relationship between Abraham and Sarah. Their marriage revolved around the child they had not been able to have, the child God had promised but had not delivered.

The same type of relational problems are critical threats to marriage in the middle years today.

It can be a crisis between husband and wife. The decrease of affection between the mates and the physical change that has already been mentioned often causes men to want to prove their virility or wives to seek affection in a third party. The addition of this third person shatters the confidence and trust that ties the couple together. Thus, the permanence of their relationship is threatened. We see this very clearly in the experience of Abraham, Sarah, and Hagar. Sarah suggested that Abraham sleep with Hagar for the purpose of producing an heir (16:2). When it happened, Sarah despised Hagar (v. 4). Hagar evidently felt superior to Sarah because she had done what Sarah could not do—she had given Abraham a son. Sarah later demanded that Abraham cast Hagar out (21:10) which Abraham did, reluctantly (v. 11). A triangular relationship never works.

These relational problems can also revolve around the children. The very presence of children in marriage often causes problems. One therapist said that he does not know a single case of middle-age divorce where the alienation had not started with the birth of the first child, the displacement of the father, his acting out his resentment, and the beginning of a long series of conflicts and tensions.[4]

Then during the middle years of marriage the children are in their teenage years. The manifold physical changes and the search for identity that teenagers go through often makes them hard to live with. The girl who wrote this letter to her father, "Daddy, I hate you," but signed it, "Love, Sarah," expressed the ambivalent emotions of the teenage years. At times, the personal crises of teenagers affect the relationships within the home.

As the children get older the weaning away process begins and the traces of the generation gap become more evident. Hostility between parents and children often grows out of this stage, leaving a dark shadow over the home.

This leads then to the child launching state which is usually most traumatic for mothers and results in what is called "the empty nest syndrome." For years the children and their activities have been the hub around which the home whirled. After they are gone, their absence demands radical readjustment on the part of parents. Many men and women, alone together again, discover that they really have nothing more in common. They have a relational problem.

In addition, there are *psychological problems*. It does not take much reading between the lines to see the psychological turmoil Abraham and Sarah were experiencing in this period of their lives. When Abraham first left Haran (Gen. 12:1), the Lord promised that he would make of him a great nation. In Genesis 12:7; 15:4; and 15:5 this promise was reaffirmed. Yet, ten years later (Gen. 16) the child had still not come, the promises had still not been fulfilled, and with the horizon of death not too far ahead Abraham and Sarah began to think that these promises never would be fulfilled. This led to hostility, doubt, disillusionment, and eventually despair. Things had not turned out as they expected.

Much the same kind of psychological dilemmas face marriage today when the twenty-year itch comes. Let me just briefly mention a few aspects of it.

One psychological dilemma could be called disillusionment. By this time a couple has gone through so much together. The mystique has evaporated, and they see each other for what they really are. This is what has led one person to say, "No man is a hero to his wife." The changes they thought would come have not. They have seen each other at their worst too many times. And if early marriage can be expressed in the phrase, "oceans of emotion surrounded by expanses of expenses," then marriage in middlescence can be expressed in the phrase, "dimensions of tension surrounded by years of tears." The surprises are gone. The result is boredom, the trauma of eventlessness, or a routine relationship in which each takes the other for granted.

One son told his father he was going to run away from home to find some excitement. The father said, "Just a minute son. I'll go with you." Disillusionment has come. Both the verbal communication lines and the sexual communication lines are often blocked leading to what one man has called the "go-away-closer disease." The husband and wife may be craving for contact and relationship with each other, but because there have been so many misunderstandings, so many disagreements, so many rebuffs, and so many hurts in the past the mates avoid contact like poison when it is offered. Longing for intimacy, they sabotage (usually unconsciously) any chance that might provide that intimacy.

The success-failure factor is involved as well. By the time of middle age we usually know about what our ultimate level of accomplishment in life will be. If we fall too short of our original goals, a sense of failure may engulf us.

The slowdown of activity and the absence of children will also provide more time to begin thinking about the meaning of life. We, like Abraham and Sarah, may see some long desired goal that eluded us and cry out in anguish, "Why did it happen? What is the real meaning of life?"

Gail Sheehy in *Passages* describes the dilemma: "If one has refused to budge through the midlife transition, the sense of staleness will calcify into resignation. One by one, the safety and supports will be withdrawn from the person who is standing still. Parents will become children; children will become strangers; a mate will grow away or go away; the career will become just a job—and each of these events will be felt as an abandonment." [5]

You may already be experiencing the physical problems, the relational problems and the psychological difficulties which are an inevitable part of marriage in the middle years. The presence of these problems, however, is not something to be ashamed of. It is not a sin. The only sin is to fail to admit that they are there and refuse to do anything about them.

The Prescription

What can be done? What is the prescription for the twenty-year itch? There are certainly no easy answers, but let me make a few suggestions.

The first step is *proper planning*. This is a word for those who have not yet reached this stage. Realize that it is going to come and get ready for it.

It has been suggested that marriage is a lottery game. Some are lucky and others are fated to be unlucky. What will be will be. It seems more accurate to liken marriage to a rare rose which if properly tended will grow into a beautiful blossom but if neglected will die. This means that it is better to keep your marriage strong and healthy along the way than to try to put it back together later on.

How can we do that? I think we need to realize that marriage is not a simple relationship based on love or sex but is a total life-embracing community that is held up by at least six different supports: love, dialogue, sexual communication, parenthood, philosophy of life, and daily life. To prepare for the twenty-year itch we must carefully develop each of these vital areas. We cannot develop one or two and leave the others undone. We must tend to them all. We prepare for the middle years when we develop our unique pattern of love, develop our emotional and personal relationship through dialogue, share the intimacies of a physical relationship, plan together the size of our family and raise the children together, develop together our practical philosophy of life, and structure together our daily life in our work and leisure time.[6]

Some have suggested "Eat, drink and be merry, for tomorrow we die" as the motto for life. For marriage, a much more fitting slogan would be, "Prepare, for tomorrow you may live." It is probable that some day you will be where Abraham and Sarah are. You need to prepare for that time.

The second step is *proper perspective*. The middle years of marriage do bring about a change. There is no question about it. We must accept it and then begin to adjust to it. Things will change, but the real threat to marriage in middlescence is not the changes but our attitudes toward the changes. It is true that we cling tenaciously to what is customary and familiar and thus resist change. However, John Henry Newman was probably right when he wrote "to live is to change, and to be perfect is to have changed often." [7] Accept the inevitability of change, recognize the changes when they come, get your perspective straight, and then you will be ready for the third step.

That is *proper patterns*, new ways of relating to each other and to life. Consider these suggestions.

1. Seek a new intimacy as a husband and wife. It will be hard at first, but it can be done. You have more time to really get to know each other now than you have ever had since courtship. Take a second honeymoon. Read some books on marriage enrichment. Get to know each other all over again.

2. Learn to intermingle your roles. The rigid separation between a man's job and woman's job in the home, when broken down, will provide more time together and will lead to a better understanding of each other. One couple made a list of all the unpleasant chores and then divided them among the husband and wife. This sharing of the bad with the good was the key that unlocked the door to a new intimacy.

3. Develop deeper relationships with friends. How? One man suggested a simple plan: to keep a friend, honor him present, praise him absent, and assist him in his necessities. Friends will provide new emotional outlets and will expand the dimension of your life.

4. Develop new relationships with your children. Being a real friend to a child after having severed the apron strings can be a richly rewarding experience. My wife and I were talking about the day when our four children will be grown and married. We wondered what kind of parents-in-law we would be. Jan said, "When the children get married, I'm going to start it off right. I am going to tell them that I'm new at being a mother-in-law just like they are new at being a daughter-in-law. So let's just try to be friends." That's a plan that will work.

5. Develop new and broader avenues for service. You have time and wisdom and skills that can be used to help other people.[8]

If you don't have the twenty-year itch yet, prepare for it because it is coming. If you get your perspective straight and then begin practicing the proper patterns, these years can be the most rewarding of your marriage.

Conclusion

A cynic once complained that marriage starts with a prince kissing an angel and ends with a bald man sitting across the table from a fat woman. The secret that eludes the cynic is that with proper planning and proper perspective and proper patterns of behavior there can be such a thing as a bald-headed prince and a slightly overweight angel. Why not see if you can discover that bald-headed prince and slightly overweight angel in your home?

3
Don't Lose the Vision

Isaac and Rebekah
Genesis 24

One of the most facinating stories in the Bible is that of Isaac and Rebekah's marriage. If there was ever a marriage made in heaven, this was it. From the commissioning of the servant to the confrontation with Rebekah at the well to the collective bargaining with the family to the consummation of the union in Isaac's tent, everything went according to plan. It was love at first sight, a marriage arranged in heaven, a union destined for success. Yet, somehow success evaded Isaac and Rebekah. They started out on the right foot, but somewhere along the line they lost the vision.

The Right Beginning

Many of the couples of the Bible are brought together with little concern for the way their lives match. The marriage of Samson and the Philistine girl is a prime example (Judg. 14), or David and Bathsheba (2 Sam. 11), or Abigail and Nabal (1 Sam. 25:3). In contrast, clearly evident in the story of Isaac and Rebekah's marriage is the careful way in which their lives were matched.

Notice that Isaac was forty years old and still not married (Gen. 25:20). The primary reason for Isaac's singleness at this point was probably the land in which he lived. The pagan girls in the land were not of the same type as Isaac. A proper partner with whom to match his life was just not available. So, rather than marrying the wrong person, Isaac remained unmarried.

Abraham took the initiative in finding Isaac a wife. He commanded his most trusted servant to find a woman suitable for Isaac to marry. The hand under the thigh, accompanied by a vow (vv. 2-3), indicated the seriousness of the matter. Abraham instructed his servant to find for his son a wife of the same religion, the same race, the same general family and social background. Abraham wanted a girl who in character and personality and background was rightly matched to his son, for he felt that a proper matching was a necessary foundation for a successful marriage. Whom a person marries does make a difference.

In recent days, there has been a reaction against this truth, a tendency to discount the importance of a proper matching. Young people often declare that the background is not important. Love will conquer all. But will love conquer all? Is a proper matching important?

Dr. Bernard Harnik, noted Swiss physician and counselor, after years of experience has concluded that marriage "within one's station" is by no means an outmoded concept. It is still valid today.[1]

Marriage "within one's station" involves a common social background. This was the value of marriages in earlier times when a person almost always found a partner from some neighboring family with whom they shared the same basic values, education, and experience. Without that a marriage can succeed, but the amount of adjustment demanded is greatly increased.[2]

A common spiritual background is also involved. Each major religious body, Protestant, Roman Catholic, and Jewish, teaches that young people ought to marry within their own faith. The reason for this is that in an interfaith marriage the couple cannot have fellowship together in the most important area of the Christian life. In-law problems are more likely in an interfaith marriage. The addition of children complicates the matter further when their religious education has to be decided. Tests have shown that the children of an interfaith marriage experience some difficulties to which children in one-faith marriages are not exposed.[3]

Albert I. Gordon, in his book on intermarriage, gives statistics which verify the importance of common social and religious backgrounds. "The statistical evidence incorporated in this study," he says, "makes it clear that the 'odds' do not favor intermarriages, in that almost two to four times as many intermarriages as intramarriages end in divorce, separation or annulment." [4]

There should also be some common interests with your proposed mate. With both partners working in most cases today, the only time a couple has to be together is in their leisure time. Without some common interests to tie them together there, a strong relationship cannot be built.

The proposed mate should be someone who will be a good companion. Compatability is not determined by your sexual prowess but by the way you relate on a day-by-day basis. If you do not marry someone with whom you can be a friend as well as a lover, you are headed for trouble.

In addition, the proposed mate should have a similar intellectual level. I'm not talking about common grade level necessarily, as if to say that college graduates should only marry college graduates and Ph.D.'s should marry only Ph.D.'s. I mean the ability to relate intellectually. You have to be able to communicate with each other on a common intellectual basis, for meaningful dialogue is essential to a lasting relationship.

How will you know all of these things beforehand? That is what the engagement period is for. It is a time to test the psychological compatibility of a man and woman, to communicate deeply about their goals and to determine if there are enough similarities to build a life together.

Of course, this does not mean that you have to be identical to your proposed mate at every point. Nothing would be so boring as a relationship between two people exactly alike. It simply means, as Abraham realized, that the more similarities there are, the more common ground there is; the more perfectly you are matched, the less traumatic will be the adjustments that have to be made and the better chance you have for a successful marriage. The matching is important.

The Wrong Ending

It is clear from the experience of Isaac and Rebekah that although a good matching is important, it is not enough. Because Isaac and Rebekah were so beautifully matched, the marriage seemed destined for success. A quick glance at the story, however, indicates that something happened. When Isaac and Rebekah first saw each other, it was love at first sight, but Genesis 27 shows them estranged and antagonistic. Somewhere along the way they lost the vision.

What happened? It is impossible to know for sure. The most likely conclusion is that Isaac and Rebekah rested on the laurels of their good beginning. They failed to face the daily challenge of building a strong relationship. They did not realize that marriage is hard work. As a foundation is only the first stage in building a house, a proper matching is only the first stage in building a marriage. As the vision began to fade for Isaac and Rebekah, they did not try to refocus it.

Dr. Harnik says that every couple goes through a critical period in their marriage sometime between the second

34

and fifth year. By that time, a certain disenchantment has settled over the marriage. The honeymoon is over and the masks have been removed. Marriage is seen for what it really is. At that point, the couple stands at a crossroads. If they refuse to acknowledge the crisis and deal with it, or if they seek to deal with it by initiating extramarital relationships, the marriage will probably fall apart. If, on the other hand, they see the crisis as an opportunity to move on to something better, to move from idealism to reality, from the honeymoon to a healthy relationship, from young love to mature love, from monologue to dialogue, from cohabitation to real unity, then they can come out of the crisis with a richer relationship and a stronger marriage than they had before.[5]

Isaac and Rebekah evidently never made it through the valley of disenchantment. Consequently, their marriage, made in heaven and destined for success, was mired in the mud of indifference. They still lived together, but their relationship was dead.

The Right Ending

Is wedlock always a padlock that leads to deadlock? Or is it possible to have a good ending? Could the disaster of Isaac and Rebekah have been avoided? The fact that many couples do get married and live happily ever after affirms the possibility. Good beginnings can be climaxed with good endings.

But how? What is the secret? Benjamin Franklin once offered this suggestion: "Keep your eyes open before marriage and half shut afterward." Cyd Charisse gave this advice to wives. "To keep your husband happy, you need to treat him like a dog—give him three meals a day, lots of affection, and a loose leash." The late Lyndon B. Johnson suggested to husbands: "To keep your wife happy two things are necessary. First, let her think she is having her way and second, let her have it."

Those suggestions are more humorous than helpful. Howard Clinebell is probably closer to the truth when he said that it takes guts to stay together and those who do are heroes. So what does it take to be a hero?

1. *Keep the search going.*—Although Isaac and Rebekah were perfectly matched, a certain aura of mystery still surrounded their marriage. When they first met, they did have some basic information about each other. Rebekah knew what the servant had told her about Isaac. Isaac knew what kind of woman the servant had been commissioned to find. So when the servant approached with the woman, Isaac automatically knew something about her religion, her character, and her family background.

They did know a little about each other. Yet, buried beneath the surface facts they did know was a whole sea of unknowns. This aura of mystery in their relationship was symbolized by the veil which Rebekah put over her face when she saw Isaac approaching (v. 65). It can be summarized in one simple sentence: "They knew so little about each other."

That aura of mystery in the marriage relationship is still a reality today. Even with a perfect match, the mystery is still there.

There is *the mystery of our different expectations.* Our understanding of marriage is shaped by what we see in our homes growing up, what we read about marriage, and what our married friends tell us. Out of all this input, every person reaches a basic understanding of what is expected of him and what he expects of his mate in marriage. The problem is that the expectations of one person will never perfectly concur with those of another. During courtship, we verbalize some of these expectations and iron out some of the differences. But there are many areas of difference which will never be discovered until the marriage relationship has begun, like who will take out the garbage, or what side of the bed you sleep on, or how you squeeze the toothpaste out of the tube, or who gets up first in the morning, or who changes the diapers. These unresolved conflicts in our expectations create a perpetual atmosphere of mystery in marriage.

There is also *the mystery of our different sexes.* E. E. LeMasters, in his book *Modern Courtship and Marriage,* distinguishes between male and female subcultures in society. He says that the process of socialization creates a subculture for each sex. Although there is some exposure to the other subculture in sibling relationships, school relationships, and courtship, the barriers between the two subcultures are never totally overcome.[6]

One young girl told her grandmother about her sweet, young boyfriend. She hinted that they might soon be married. Her grandmother pointed out that in almost every area the boy was different from her. The young girl said, "Grandma, don't you know that opposites attract?" Grandmother responded, "Just being boy and girl is opposite enough." She was right! There is a vast difference between a man and a woman, woman's lib notwithstanding. As eminent a scholar as Paul Tournier has concluded that never can a man completely understand a woman and vice versa.[7] Thus, the mystery persists.

There is also *the mystery of the marriage union.* Marriage is a process by which we leave one family unit and begin another. Yet, we maintain a relationship with both. One of the most beautiful expressions of this process is the unity candle often used in weddings today. Two outside candles, representing the individuality of the bride and groom, are lighted at the beginning of the ceremony. At the end, these two are used to light the center candle representing unity. All three candles remain aglow. What a picture of marriage! The man and woman have become one. Yet they are still two different individuals. The unity does not remove the individuality. The existence of the new family does not erase the reality or the memory of the old. In this kind of relationship where $1 + 1 = 1$ and $1 + 1 = 2$ are both correct, a degree of mystery is inevitable.

Even with a perfect matching and a long courtship, the mystery persists. It was true of Isaac and Rebekah. It is true of every marriage. The ancient Hebrews recognized this fact. When a young man married, he was released from all his responsibilities for a full year so he could give undivided attention to exploring the mysterious caverns of his new relationship and come to know this person to whom he had committed his life (Deut. 24:5).

You'll never completely remove the mystery of your marriage. You'll never completely understand your mate. So keep the search going.

2. *Keep the communication flowing.*—Have you ever watched people when you go out to eat? Try to determine which couples are married and which are not. What is your clue? It's simple. The ones who are talking are not married.

One wife complained that her husband spent three hours talking to strangers on his CB, but he would not even say good morning to her. Can you identify with that?

We'll deal with the matter of communication in chapter 6, but it is worth repeating that communication is one of the vital keys to a happy marriage. Communication leads to understanding and understanding leads to happiness in the home.

3. *Keep the love showing.*—Picture a scene in a typical family room. The wife, with a tear starting to form in the corner of her eye, looks at her husband. "Honey,"

she says, "you haven't told me you loved me in a long time." "Listen," he returns, "I told you once and if I change my mind I'll let you know."

What a misconception of love! Love will not grow automatically. It has to be nourished. If it is nourished it will grow, but if neglected it will die. Love in marriage is nourished by a constant recreation of that which caused it to happen in the first place.

David Mace points out a change in the marriage relationship today. In the past, marriage was held together by external coercion. Community morals and religious morals were against divorce. Thus, couples were coerced to stay together even when the love had died. Today much of that external coercion has eroded. Divorce has become accepted and acceptable in most communities. Religious leaders are less concerned now in condemning divorce than in strengthening marriages before divorce and ministering to the broken families after divorce. So the external coercion has been removed. Now, the motivation for staying together has to come from an internal cohesion.[8] That is why it is so important to nourish your love. How can you nourish your love?

Value it. Instead of wishing you were married to someone else, focus on the positive qualities in your mate that makes you fortunate to have him/her. The key to a happy marriage is not finding the right person but keeping the right attitude. The couple who made a list of each other's virtues, framed the list, and hung it in their bedroom as a daily reminder, had discovered the secret of valuing their love.

Verbalize it. Take time to express your love. Try saying, "I love you" when you aren't wanting something from your mate.

Visualize it. "Actions speak louder than words" may be trite, but it is also true. "I love you" is an empty cliché unless it is followed by actions of love. Surprise gifts, special nights out, volunteering to help with an unpleasant chore—these are ways of visualizing your love. One man sent his wife eleven roses with a note which said, "You are the twelfth rose." Don't you know that he got his message across?

4. *Keep the vision glowing.*—There are three steps to making a marriage strong: remember it like it was, face it like it is, and imagine it the way it can be. There was a time in your relationship when you first envisioned what life could be like together with the person you loved. You envisioned a relationship that would last forever, one that would bring joy and fulfillment. Maintaining the vision is a vital part of a successful marriage.

Elton Trueblood has beautifully expressed it: "A successful marriage is not one in which two people, beautifully matched, find each other and get along happily ever after because of this initial matching. It is, instead, a system by means of which persons who are sinful and contentious are so caught up by a dream bigger than themselves that they work throughout the years, in spite of repeated disappointments, to make the dream come true."[9]

So whatever you do, don't lose the vision.

4

Love at Second Sight

Jacob and Leah
Genesis 29:29 to 30:24

The marriage of Jacob and Leah was an accident that grew into a blessing. It was not what Jacob planned, for he fell in love at first with ravishing Rachel. He agreed to work seven years for her after which she would become his wife. The biblical writer, with a romantic flair, declares of those seven years: "they seemed to him but a few days because of his love for her" (Gen. 29:20). Finally the wedding day arrived. The wine flowed abundantly so that by the time the celebration was over Jacob was drunk. He then took his fully veiled bride into the darkness of the honeymoon chamber and, in a half-drunken stupor, their marriage was consummated. But the next morning Jacob was shocked into soberness! Verse 25 expresses the startling discovery in classic words: "In the morning . . . behold, it was Leah!"

Jacob later married Rachel also, and these three lived together for many years in a tempestuous, ticklish triangle. But before Rachel became his wife and after Rachel was dead, Jacob's primary relationship was with Leah. As much as is possible I want us to forget about Rachel and concentrate on the relationship between Jacob and Leah.

The Dark Side

The first discovery we make is that there were several things which were wrong about the marriage of Jacob and Leah. This is the dark side of the picture.

The marriage of Jacob and Leah obviously had a *wrong beginning*. It was based entirely on deception. The only reason that Jacob married Leah at all was that he had been trapped in a carefully planned scheme devised by her father. In an ironic twist, Jacob the deceiver is deceived. The story of his deception of Isaac in order to obtain the blessing which rightfully belonged to Esau is told in Genesis 27. Now Jacob received similar treatment from Rebekah's brother, Laban. It is not clear what Leah's part was in the deception, but she was at least a willing participant. It could be that she was desperate to get married and she saw this as her last chance. The relationship between Jacob and Leah began on the shabbiest of foundations—dishonesty and deception.

It is sad but true that there are many marriages today which are based on the same shaky foundation. People often get married without really knowing their mate because they have so deceptively disguised themselves. Some of the deception is, of course, unconscious. For instance, during the courtship period we naturally put our best foot forward. We are not being deliberately deceptive. We just emphasize the brighter side of our personality, subtly camouflaging the shadows, to make ourselves more appealing. All of us do that. In addition, there are some personality characteristics and personal expectations about marriage that are never discussed. It is not that we deliberately avoid discussing these things. Often we just do not think of them.

That is why a long courtship is so important. It provides the opportunity to fully explore the feelings and desires and expectations in the deepest recesses of your being. It promotes a security in which you can begin taking down the masks and really be yourself. And it prevents the kind of deception which is expressed so vividly in our text. Jacob and Leah most certainly started on the wrong foot for their marriage was based on deliberate deception.

We also see that Jacob married the *wrong bride*. It is difficult for us to understand how this could have happened. When we remember the different customs of courtship which prevailed in that day, the high level of intoxication caused by the celebration, and the lack of adequate lighting, it all begins to make more sense. Explain it or not, the fact remains that it happened. For seven years Jacob had labored for, and longed for the beautiful, shapely Rachel. But when he woke up the next morning he found that he had married her weak-eyed sister, Leah. By "weak-eyed" (v. 17) the biblical writer does not mean that she could not see well. He means she lacked the luster, the sparkle, that gleamed in the eyes of Rachel. Translated into today's terms, it means she looked like she had been whipped by an ugly stick! She was not the girl of his dreams. He had married the wrong girl.

This is evidently the experience of many married people today. Dr. Harnik says that it is usually during the second maturing crisis, after having been married for about eighteen years, that the husband or wife begins to regret having married the person they have rather than someone else who now seems more desirable.[1] It may be this and not the empty nest syndrome which causes an increasing number of divorces in this age group.

I believe that it happens earlier than that. There are many people who after their first year of marriage, even after their honeymoon, feel that the person they married does not really fit their long cherished ideal and they are haunted by the feeling that they have married the wrong person.

What is the source of this feeling?

Sometimes this feeling is caused by a distorted model.

For so long, especially from the pulpit, we have idealized the marriage relationship. We have led people to believe that the wedding ceremony is a gateway into a rose garden of uninterrupted bliss where we will live happily ever after. We forget that it is, instead, a relationship between two people whose differences will continually cause conflicts that have to be handled. We idealize marriage. When our marriage fails to meet the ideal, when the conflicts begin, we conclude that we must have married the wrong person. If we had married the right person, we would not be having these problems.

Sometimes the feeling that we married the wrong person is caused by a distorted perspective. This tendency to see the grass on the other side of the fence as always being a little greener than ours was discussed in chapter 1. Viewed from the outside, many marriages seem to be happier than ours. The difference is not really in the marriage, however. It is in the perspective from which we view it. The irony is that many times the couples we envy look at our marriage with the same kind of envy and longing.

The feeling may be caused by a distorted evaluation of ourselves. Sometimes we just think we deserved a better deal. On their honeymoon a certain groom took his bride by the hand and said, "Now that we're married, dear, I hope you won't mind if I mention a few little defects I've noticed about you." "Not at all," she said with deceptive sweetness, "It was those little defects that kept me from getting a better husband." When we refuse to admit those little defects, we feel like we deserve better.

Jacob entered marriage thinking that he was marrying Rachel. But when he woke up in the morning, behold, it was Leah. He married the wrong bride.

Notice also that they practiced the *wrong behavior*. Look at the Scripture passage. You will discover that

Leah and Rachel and Jacob were constantly at each other's throat, trying to gain control of the situation, trying to win affection. The obvious fact that Jacob loved Rachel more than Leah (v. 30) led to constant competition. When Leah bore a son for Jacob, she hoped that this would make Jacob love her more (v. 32). This son was followed with three more sons. They were trophies with which Leah hoped to gain the affection of her husband.

These events produced no affection in Rachel, however. In her jealousy she decided to allow Jacob to sleep with her handmaid so she could have children through her. As if two wives were not enough! The handmaid bore two sons which led Rachel to conclude: "With great wrestlings have I wrestled with my sister, and I have prevailed" (Gen. 30:8, KJV).

Then Leah got into the act. She persuaded Jacob to sleep with her handmaid. Now Jacob had a quartet of women to contend with. On and on the struggle went between Jacob, his two wives, and their handmaids. Instead of a reciprocal relationship of affection, acceptance, and association, Leah and Jacob and Rachel were involved in a power struggle.

In most marriages today, even when a third party is not involved, there is the same kind of power struggle going on between a husband and a wife.

In his book, *Games People Play,* Eric Berne has a special section on marital games, games husbands and wives play. With great insight he discusses the various approaches husbands and wives use in the power struggle.[2] A close look at this discussion will reveal insights into marital conflict through such games as the frigid woman, the harried housewife, the miserly money manager, and others.

Let me illustrate how a couple of these marital games work. One example is the unsatisfied wife. There is nothing that her husband can do to please her. As hard as he tries, she remains dissatisfied. What the wife is doing is using her dissatisfaction to perpetuate a feeling of guilt in her husband. This gives her the upper hand in the power struggle.

There is the "hen-pecked husband" routine, the man who constantly flails his wife with the idea that she never lets him have any time to go out with the boys. He creates the same kind of guilt that the dissatisfied wife creates, thus moving the power to his side.

The games go on and on. Although one expert on the home says that women usually fight on the sexual level and men on the financial level, anything can be used in the power struggle: your children, your knowledge, your physical attractiveness. Anything!

Marriage is supposed to be a relationship of mutual trust, caring cohabitation, and reciprocal responsibility. But when we make of marriage a power struggle in which we constantly play games to gain the upper hand, then we, like Leah and Jacob, are participating in unhealthy marriage behavior.

Unlike the marriage of Isaac and Rebekah which began on a firm foundation, with everything going for them, in the marriage of Jacob and Leah everything seemed to be wrong at the beginning.

The Bright Side

But there is also a bright side. This is the good news. The amazing discovery as we follow through on the story is that this marriage which started out so weak really ended up strong. In the end, there were also some right things about the relationship of Jacob and Leah.

This is implied as we follow through on the story in Genesis. The panic with which Rachel reacted in Genesis 30:1 implies that Leah and Jacob had established a solid relationship by this time which threatened Rachel's position. In Genesis 31:4, when Jacob prepared to leave Laban, he took both Leah and Rachel into his confidence, which implies an equality of concern for both. In Genesis 49:31 we see that it was Leah who was buried in Machpelah, the family sepulcher bought by Abraham, alongside Jacob. This, too, implies an honored position for her.

When we remember further that it was from the relationship of Jacob and Leah, not Jacob and Rachel, that the messianic line was continued (through Judah), we realized that although this marriage started out with seemingly no hope it turned out to be a healthy, happy relationship.

There are two lessons here for us.

Bad beginnings can be overcome. Honesty would compel many of you to admit your marriage started off on the wrong foundation. Maybe the person you married was really your second choice. Maybe you are your mate's second choice. Maybe you did not get to have the kind of wedding you wanted. Maybe your parents seriously objected. Maybe there was an unwanted pregnancy involved. If the experience of Jacob and Leah tells us anything it is that bad beginnings can be overcome.

I know a couple who began their marriage with everything against them. The bride was only fourteen and was pregnant. Neither of the parents were able to give financial aid, and at eighteen the boy was unprepared to provide for a family. They giggled all the way through their wedding to keep from crying. They were facing a stacked deck. What happened since then? For fifteen years the marriage has not only lasted but has flourished. The girl, who earned her high school degree, is a fine mother and supportive wife. The man, who finished college and law school, is doing well in his profession. They love each other dearly. They have a strong home. Bad beginnings can be overcome!

Love can be created. When Jacob and Leah married there was no love at all. Over the years, however, a quality of love was developed. What they discovered is that marriage was not the result of love, but the opportunity for love.

This is probably what Mark Twain had in mind when he said, "Love seems the swiftest, but it is the slowest of all growths. No man, or woman, really knows what perfect love is until they have been married a quarter of a century." [3]

Rabindranath Tagore said much the same thing with his comparison between American and Indian marriages. American marriage is a hot pot and a cold stove burner, he said. The couple is hot at marriage, but they soon cool off. In India it is the opposite. India marriage is a cold pot and a hot stove burner. The Indians do not marry for love, but as soon as they are married, love begins to grow.[4]

So many today declare that you can fall out of love after you are married. What I am saying is that you can also fall in love after you are married. How can it happen?

1. It begins with a right attitude. The most important factor in a successful marriage is not finding the right person but finding and keeping the right attitude. The couple I alluded to earlier succeeded, even after a bad start, because they were determined to do it.

2. It takes hard work. Mickey Rooney once suggested that any person who says marriage is a fifty-fifty proposition either does not understand marriage or does not know fractions. Marriage at its best demands two people at their best giving their best. No fifty-fifty will do. Each must give 100 percent.

3. Prayer will help. Charlie Shedd says that out of two thousand cases covering twenty years of counseling he has never had one couple or one member of a marriage come to him with their troubles if they prayed together.[5]

4. Forgiveness is essential. No other human relationship engenders as much anger as marriage. Mistakes will be made. Hurts will be felt. But a daily dose of "I'm sorry" and "I forgive you," genuinely expressed, is the best prescription to keep that anger from developing into smouldering grudges.

Conclusion

Jacob loved Rachel at first sight. But he seems to have loved Leah at second sight. I do not mean that in the way one girl expressed it. She said she fell in love at second sight because the first time she looked she didn't know the guy was rich. I mean, rather, that when Jacob took a deeper look, when he penetrated beneath the surface, he discovered in Leah a quality with which he could relate. This allowed their relationship which seemed doomed to failure to turn out all right in the end.

There are, no doubt, some unpleasant factors in your marriage. You can see the dark side, the shadows. But I want to challenge you to look on the bright side. Whatever has happened before, bad beginnings can be overcome, love can be created, a strong relationship can be developed, and you, too, can fall in love at second sight.

5

⸱ Married but Discontented

Othniel and Achsah
Joshua 15:16-19

Larry Christenson cites a survey in which 77 percent of the women who responded said they would rather not be married.[1] That many are unhappy in their marriage is undeniable. Nor does it surprise us when it appears in the later years of marriage, as in Abraham and Sarah, or in a couple like Isaac and Rebekah, who moved through the early maturing crisis unsuccessfully. But unhappy on the honeymoon! That is surprising.

This is exactly what we find in the relationship of Achsah and Othniel. If ever there was a time when Achsah should have been happy, this was it. She had just married Othniel, one of the bravest young men in her tribe. The nephew of Caleb, Othniel was to rise to heights of fame in Israel. He was one of the dynamic leaders called judges who judged Israel and prevailed over the oppressors. He was quite a catch! In addition, Achsah had been given a dowry of valuable southland from her father. Achsah and Othniel were in the honeymoon period and a bright future was before them. Achsah should have been hilariously happy. Instead, this brief scriptural cameo shows her to be very discontented.

Why? There were two obvious reasons, although other reasons might have been at work beneath the surface. This bride of yesteryear reflects in her life two characteristic attitudes which are at the root of most marital discontent today.

Conceit

The first of these unhealthy attitudes is conceit—the love of self. Here was a woman whose world revolved around herself. She didn't just think she was valuable. She thought she was priceless. Achsah entered marriage with the idea that she was a princess whose every want was to be immediately fulfilled by her husband. She was born to be a queen.

It is easy to discover how this understanding developed. Her name connoted something special. Her name means "adorned" and speaks of the physical beauty which was hers from birth and the special pampering she received from her parents. In addition, 1 Chronicles 4:15 indicates that she was the only daughter in a family with three adoring, protecting brothers. What's more, she was set up as a prize for the man who was courageous enough to capture the city of Kiriath-sepher for her father, Caleb.

Here was a bride who all of her life was told she was beautiful, who was coddled and spoiled by three adoring brothers, and was set up as a special prize for the bravest man in her tribe. Is it any wonder she thought she was a princess? She entered marriage with herself upon a pedestal. The basic purpose of marriage in her eyes was to fulfill her needs.

This attitude is at the heart of most problem marriages today. Call it conceit or love of self or selfishness. It is ever present. We have put ourselves and our desires at the center of our marriage.

In Greek mythology there was a handsome young man named Narcissus who one day happened to see his reflection in a still pool of water. He became so infatuated with himself that he was unable to pull away from admiring his face in the pool. From that piece of folklore the psychologists have taken the term "narcissistic" and used it to refer to any extreme form of self-admiration. It is becoming evident that our society is increasingly moving in the direction of narcissism.

Dr. Raymond Baumhart, president of Loyola University of Chicago, recently stated that "selfishness has become an American characteristic." [2] Social critic Tom Wolfe calls the 1970s the "me decade." Frank Sinatra influenced an entire generation to do it "my way." One of the leaders of the *New York Times* best seller's list in 1977 was *Looking Out for Number One.* The basic thesis of the book is, "You have to spend time concentrating on making yourself happy."

This narcissistic obsession with self-fulfillment and self-contentment has carried over into marriage where husbands and wives have begun to make "looking out for number one" their number one priority. Selfishness! An egocentric greed for fulfilling experience! That is at the heart of our problems in marriage today.

Why is such self-love a problem in marriages?

To begin with, it establishes *an impossible goal* for marriage. The idea of complete self-fulfillment is a myth. It cannot happen. We are multifaceted in our character and in our moods. To expect some other individual to match every mood, satisfy every demand, and fulfill all of our needs is unrealistic. Thus, to set up as a goal for your marriage complete self-fulfillment in which every need is met is to condemn yourself to a life of perpetual discontent or to relegate yourself to an unending search for the perfect partner.

There are going to be times in your marriage when your needs are not met, when you do not feel fulfilled. The answer is not to find another partner, nor to wallow in self-pity at your plight. The answer is what one man has called "creative fidelity." [3] This is the ability to maintain commitment to a marriage during those dry periods when one's needs are not being met, to bear with your partner in his/her plateaus, regression, and imperfections in such a way that these are transformed into new possibilities.

In addition, extreme narcissism establishes *an improper goal* for your marriage. Selfishness declares that the purpose of marriage is to fulfill "my" needs, but there is more to a marriage than just meeting your needs. You and your mate both have heart-hungers that marriage was created to fulfill. The key to a successful marriage is not what you are getting out of it, but what you are putting into it. The approach that Jesus suggests is not "Give me" but "Give, and it shall be given unto you." That's true of marriage as it is about every other area of your life. Instead of waiting to get your needs filled you need to start filling the needs of your partner.

This is not to deny the fact that we all have needs. We do. We all have basic heart-hungers which must be met. These emotional needs are beautifully described by Dorothy W. Baruch: "We need *love* in good measure, and we need to give it. We need to feel that we are *wanted and belong*. We need to feel that we are capable of *adequate* achievement so we can manage to meet life's demands. We need *recognition* for what we achieve. We need to know that the *pleasure which our senses and our body can bring us* is permissible and good and that our enjoyment does not make us 'bad.' We need to feel accepted and understood. And finally, we need to feel *worthwhile and essentially worthy in being uniquely the self that we are.*"[4] Nor do I deny that the purpose of marriage is, in part, to satisfy these needs. I simply want us to get our perspectives right. There are two approaches to our needs.

You can approach marriage from the stance, "Marriage is to meet my needs." Most marriages consist of two people looking out for their own self-interest, seeking the fulfillment of their own needs. The result is that no one is satisfied.

There is another perspective from which to approach marriage and that is from the needs of your mate. "The purpose of marriage is for me to meet his needs" is what this perspective will lead the wife to say. "I want to do everything possible to satisfy her" is what this perspective will lead the husband to say. The result, in this case, will be a reciprocal reaction of love, tenderness, and concern which will lead to ultimate fulfillment for both partners. It is a matter of perspective.

A healthy step in the right direction for your marriage would be the honest confession to your mate, "I'm sorry I have been thinking about my needs first. I'm sorry I have been selfish. I know you have needs that I can fulfill, and beginning today I am going to commit myself to filling them." Because at the heart of marital discontent is conceit—love of self.

Covetousness

The second unhealthy attitude that Achsah reflects is covetousness—love of silver. Evidently Caleb had given to the young couple a piece of the southland for a dowry. It wasn't easy for a young couple to get started, so Caleb gave them a piece of land. But notice how Achsah responded.[5] Instead of being grateful she told Othniel, "It's not enough. Go ask him (Caleb) for something more." Othniel evidently refused, either from fear of his father-in-law or from the feeling that it would be improper. So Achsah took the matter into her own hands. She jumped on her donkey and went to Caleb with this demand, "You have given me a southland. Give me also springs of water."

The key words are "give me also" and they reflect

54

the basic covetousness of Achsah. She had an obsession with material things and an insatiable desire for more. Achsah was like one engaged lady of our day who broke her engagement and refused to marry her fiance for what she called "religious reasons." He was broke, and she worshiped money! There are a lot of people in our day who worship money.

This insatiable desire for more is at the heart of most problem marriages today. One Reno judge estimated that nine tenths of the divorces he had to contend with were over money.[6] Robert O. Blood says that "the chief cause of conflict in American families, Christian or non-Christian, is the use of money." [7]

Manuel Scott calls this insatiable desire for money "thingafication." Chrysostom, a few centuries before, called it "being nailed to the things of this life." Our forefathers called it keeping up with the Joneses. Our modern age calls it trying to get ahead. The Bible calls it covetousness. This covetousness, which was reflected in Achsah's "give me more," is the prevailing attitude in many of today's homes.

Why is it wrong? Why does the Bible condemn covetousness?

For one thing, covetousness *blurs our value system*. It leads us to believe there is nothing more important in life than money. Thus, it causes us to accept money as the end in life rather than the means to a greater end which is to glorify God and serve his kingdom.

Money, of course, is necessary for life. We all know that. To say otherwise would be foolish. The Bible never says there is anything wrong with money. It is the love of money, the Bible says, which "is the root of all evil" (1 Tim. 6:10, KJV). The Bible does not say that it is a sin to have money. It is a sin when the money has you. Jesus says that there are things more important in life than money. "Take heed, and beware of covetousness," he said, "for a man's life consisteth not in the abundance of the things which he possesseth" (Luke 12:15, KJV). On his scale of values, it is way down the list.

It is all right to have money and the things money can buy. But it is good every once in a while to check and make sure you have the things that money cannot buy.

Covetousness also begets credit buying. Proverbs 15:27 says, "He that is greedy of gain troubleth his own house" (KJV). Nowhere is this more true than in the homes where a couple has overextended themselves through unwise spending practices and excessive use of credit. The most recent figures I have seen indicate that the average American makes $13,847 a year, needs $14,333, and is in hock for $16,800.

Covetousness is extreme yearning power. When our yearning power exceeds our earning power, the only outlet seems to be the charge card. The result is that some authorities in the consumer field estimate that one third of the young families in America are only one paycheck away from bankruptcy.[8]

One man told his wife, "We are going to start living within our budget if we have to borrow to do it." Another man refused to report it when his wife's credit cards were stolen. He figured the thief would spend less than his wife! There is a new perfume on the market which smells like a credit card which is selling like crazy.

Because we have seen the credit card as the avenue for obtaining all the things that we want but cannot afford, the great challenge facing Christian couples today is not to act our age, but to start acting our wage.

In addition, *covetousness breeds discontent.* The Bible says in Ecclesiastes 5:10, "He that loveth silver shall not be satisfied with silver" (KJV). Why? Because you never get to the point where you have enough. Epicurus, the old Greek philosopher, said, "To whom little is not enough, nothing is enough." If you make $14,000 you drive yourself with the thought, "Just think of all the things we could have if I made $16,000." Then when you reach that plateau you say, "Just think what we could have if I made $20,000." The process never ends. A covetous couple is never happy because they are never satisfied. They never have enough. They always want more.

Even worse, *covetousness belittles Christian stewardship*. Jesus said on one occasion, "Every one to whom much is given, of him will much be required" (Luke 12:48, RSV). On another occasion he put it this way, "Give, and it will be given to you; good measure, pressed down, shaken together, running over, will be put into your lap" (Luke 6:38, RSV). Jesus says that the secret to a life of overabundance is to give. Covetousness says that the secret to overabundance is to "get all you can, can all you get, sit on the lid, and poison the rest."

Covetousness blurs our value system, begets unhealthy buying practices, breeds discontent, and belittles Christian stewardship. That's why family experts conclude that the chief cause of conflict in the home today is money. An infatuation for the tangible things of the world is a pathway that ends in despair.

What is the solution for money problems? One pastor suggests a fourfold solution: spend carefully, save regularly, give generously, and plan diligently.[9] John Bisagno offers these suggestions: (1) keep money in its proper perspective; (2) take out sufficient life insurance; (3) make the decision about your responsibility to God to tithe; (4) watch credit buying.[10]

I believe that the antidote for covetousness is a recommitment to God's plan for your money. What does this mean?

1. Make Christ Lord over all of your life. The Bible says that Jesus came, lived, died, and was raised for one purpose—to become the "Lord both of the dead and of the living" (Rom. 14:9). Jesus Christ wants to be the Lord over your life. He wants to call the shots. But he will never be Lord over your life until you make him Lord over your money.

2. Acknowledge God as the owner of everything you have and yourself as his trustee. God not only is in charge of your life. He owns it. The Bible says we as Christians "have been bought with a price" (1 Cor. 6:20). We no longer are our own. We belong to him. That should change our perspective on our money. Instead of trying to decide how much of our money we can give to God we now decide how much of God's money we need to keep for ourselves.

3. Discover God's purpose for every material possession of your life. A century ago Washington Gladden preached a sermon entitled "Knowing How to Be Rich" in which he proclaimed this great truth: "The first thing for any man to do who has large wealth in his hands is to put himself into right relations with that Silent Partner from whom all this abundance comes, and find out what his purposes are in regard to it. Nothing is right with him till this main question is settled." [11]

Conclusion

Is your home a happy home? Are you a contented couple? If not, it may be because one or both of you are reflecting these unhealthy attitudes that Achsah reflected: conceit (love of self) or covetousness (love of silver).

The challenge is to get self off the throne of your marriage and commit yourself to the goal of mutual need fulfillment. And then remove silver from the throne and commit yourself to God's principles for Christian stewardship. There will be no joy in your home, no contentment in your soul, until you do.

6

A Crisis in Communication

Samson and "Phylis"

Judges 14:1-20

It is a paradox, yet I have witnessed it over and over again. Without fail, the couples I deal with in premarital counseling claim to be good communicators. "We talk about everything" is the inevitable answer they give to the question, "How well do you communicate with each other?" Yet, give those couples five years and they will be singing a different song. I occasionally lead a "Couple's Clinic" in my church with about five couples. The clinic is a five-session, in-depth reexamination of marriage. I have yet to have a couple in one of these clinics who does not admit a deficiency in their communication. Evidently, sometime in the first few years a communication problem often develops.

Long before the lack of communication precipitated a crisis in marriage in our day, it was the key culprit in dividing a couple of yesteryear. Samson was the husband's name. His wife was an unnamed Philistine girl whom we will call "Phylis."

Their marriage should never have been in the first place, for it was based on simple physical attraction. When Samson saw Phylis, he told his parents: "Get her; . . . for she pleaseth me well" (v. 3, KJV). What did Samson mean? He meant that she physically appealed to him. He didn't even talk to the girl until verse 7 and by then he already had the wedding planned! Samson wanted to

60

marry Phylis simply because she made his heart go flip-flop when he saw her.

Notice also the differences between Samson and Phylis. He was an Israelite; she a Philistine. Samson had been a Nazarite from birth, indicating his consecration to a special task for God. Phylis evidently did not even share his faith in God.

There is another indication of trouble in verses 10-11. Apparently none of Samson's family were at the wedding, except for his parents, and none of his friends. Even the best man was a Philistine. What does this mean? It indicates a total rejection of the marriage arrangement by all of Samson's friends and family.

Despite this faulty foundation, the marriage could still have made it were it not for the communication crisis that arose.

The Problems

Where did Samson and Phylis go wrong? A quick glance at the story will indicate two primary problems.

At times *they talked too little*. Samson and Phylis participated in the favorite of the games couples play—the silent game. Verse 19 vividly paints the picture: "And his anger was kindled, and he went up to his father's house"(KJV). What destroys a marriage is not anger, but a refusal to deal with the problem which produces the anger. Instead of communicating about the problem, Samson went his way and Phylis went her way. They refused to communicate and the marriage died.

Ironically, another part of their communication problem was that they *talked too much*. Phylis did, that is. Samson presented a riddle to the friends of Phylis. "Out of the eater came forth meat, and out of the strong came forth sweetness"(v.14, KJV). The riddle came to Samson

61

when he noticed bees who had set up residence in the carcass of a lion he had killed. Samson delighted in the fact that the Philistines could not solve the riddle, but it angered the Philistines. They persuaded Phylis to discover the meaning of it from Samson, which she did. Then she immediately shared it with them. It was a breach of trust, for Phylis told her friends something that should have been an intimate secret between her and Samson.

Everyone needs a confidant, someone with whom he or she can share those deepest and most intimate feelings and thoughts without the fear of their being repeated. This is part of what marriage provides. When you begin sharing the confidences of intimacy with others, you are taking a step that will bring communication in your marriage to a screeching halt. Mark it down! Some things should never go beyond your front door.

Faulty communication was the heart of Samson and Phylis's problem. And it still is today. In my own counseling experience I have become aware of a crisis of communication in the home. Why is there so little communication going on in marriage?

The *complexity of the process* sometimes prevents communication. Dr. John Drakeford shows that the communication process involves seven possible distortion points. Communication originates in the information source, is encoded, comes out the transmitter, travels through the channel, is caught by the receiver, goes through the decoder, and finally arrives at the destination.[1] Disruption at any point can prevent proper communication.

Did you ever play the game called "gossip"? Everyone sits in a circle and the leader whispers a message in someone's ear. The message is repeated to each person in turn, and the final participant announces the message. The final message is not at all like the original. Why? Because the message becomes distorted as it moves along the channels from point of origin to destination. This is a practical illustration of what Drakeford was describing. Communication is a complex process. If a couple fails to develop their communication skills, neglects to provide a proper atmosphere where communication can occur, and refuses to work at it, proper communication will not occur.

Fear of criticism is another deterrent to communication. Words spoken are open to scrutiny and thus to criticism. It seems so much easier to be critical than encouraging. Somewhere in Europe there is a monument to a mule. It contains this inscription, "This is a monument to Maggie the Mule. She kicked one general, two colonels, four lieutenants, three sergeants, twenty privates, and one bomb." Some people are always kicking, pouring cold water on other people's enthusiasm.

At other times communication is cut off because of a *fear of misunderstanding*. Most words have various meanings, and often the listener attributes a different meaning to a word than the speaker intended. This is why Charlie Shedd suggests a practice he calls "saying it back." Before you respond to your partner, you repeat what he or she said to you. When the message is clear, then proper response can be given.[2]

Such a practice will help. Even more important is to keep the proper perspective. A patient once told Dr. Tournier, the eminent psychiatrist, "With you I can open up because you understand me." "No," Dr. Tournier returned, "You have it backwards. I can understand you because you open up."[3] If fear of being misunderstood is the stop sign to your communication, remember that communication is the one avenue that will lead to understanding.

Inattention to nonverbal factors also deters communication. Sterling Ellsworth, a noted counselor, suggests that communication occurs through three mediums: our body posture, our tone of voice, and our words.[4] Our words, which seem primary, are only 7 percent of the communication process. Thirty-eight percent of communication is related through our tone of voice and 55 percent through body language. That means that a person who only pays attention to the words while ignoring the tone and body language is missing the largest part of communication!

Another reason communication is avoided is *fear of conflict*. One couple told me that after fifteen years of marriage each knew exactly what would lead to conflict. When the danger point was approached, one of them would clam up or draw back to avoid the conflict. They would rather have peace than open the possibility of conflict. But peace at that price is too expensive, for David Mace states that conflict is an essential part of any growing relationship. He says we have only two choices: accept and face conflict, or live in a shallow relationship.[5] Many, however, prefer peace to penetration, so they opt for silence rather than participating in communication in depth.

There is another fear that blocks communication, *the fear of being given advice*. When we share our problems, our mate often retorts with advice that does not really take into consideration the complexity of the problem. It may be a wife who advises her husband that his problems at work would be solved if he would just take up for himself. Or it may be a husband who responds to his wife's tale of trauma in the neighborhood with a flippant, "that's a stupid thing to worry about. You're just too sensitive." [6]

The *blight of busyness* is also a problem. A woman once told her psychiatrist, "My husband is a mysterious island. I am forever circling around it but I never find a beach where I may land." How does that happen to a husband and wife? It happens when we become so preoccupied with our job, our friends, our children, our hobbies, and even our church that we do not have time to talk.

One final problem needs to be mentioned: *laziness.* Let's face it, communication is hard work. It doesn't happen automatically, but rather requires great effort. Many husbands and wives simply do not want to pay the price real communication demands.

This discussion is not exhaustive but it is suggestive. Do you have a communication problem in your marriage and wonder why? Here is a checklist:

1. Are you not developing communication skills?
2. Are you afraid of criticism?
3. Are you concerned that you will be misunderstood?
4. Are you ignoring the nonverbal factors?
5. Are you afraid of possible conflict?
6. Are you hesitant because you do not want a barrage of advice?
7. Are you too busy?
8. Are you not putting out enough effort?

The Principles

So what do you do to correct the problem of communication in your marriage? Admit it! That's the first step. And then face it head-on. Samson and Phylis gave up. They refused to face their problem head-on. But if you will dare to deal with the communication crisis in your marriage, there are some principles to keep in mind.

Be open to each other. Reuel L. Howe says, "If there is any one indispensable insight with which a young couple should begin their life together, it is that they should try to keep open, at all cost, the lines of communication between them." [7] As many barriers as possible should be removed so that the communication can flow freely between you.

Be positive with each other. Honesty with love is the key to successful communication. There is a kind of brutal frankness which is more destructive than helpful. The marriage license is not a license to insult. Rather, the marriage license provides the freedom to positively encourage, build up, and strengthen the life of your mate.

Charlie Shedd suggests starting a compliment club in every marriage. Every week the husband and wife would pay each other a compliment, sometimes a big compliment, sometimes a small one. "I like you because . . ." is a good way to begin a fruitful conversation.[8]

As a part of my counseling procedure I have the couple do a communication exercise to get the positive words flowing. I have them list and then share with each other five positive things about their mate.

I heard of one couple who made a list of these positive things, put them in a neat little frame, and hung them up in their bedroom. They agreed to read them at least once a day!

When someone pats us on our ego, especially the one closest to us in life, it will open us up and get the communication flowing.

Be a listener. This is one of the real problem spots, isn't it? How often we miss what our mate is saying to us because we are so busy deciding what we are going to say when we get our chance. Listening in-depth is a key to communication in depth.

John Wesley was strongly drawn to an eighteen-year-old girl named Sophy Hopkey, the daughter of the Chief Magistrate of Savannah. In a letter to his mother Wesley revealed why he was so attracted to her. "Another thing I was much pleased with her was that whenever we were conversing, there was a stillness about her whole behavior, scarce stirring hand or foot, that she seemed to be, all but her attention, dead." She gave Wesley her undivided attention. She listened. Thus, Wesley wanted to spend more and more time with her.[9]

Learn to listen! When someone is talking, try to determine what he is saying, what he means, and what this reveals about his feelings.

Learn to communicate in new ways. There are many ways to say I love you: a smile, a call from the office, a surprise gift, a special night out on the town, a wink across a crowded room, a gentle touch, a note left where it can be found during the day. Just as the sound of an orchestra of musicians is so much richer than the music from a single horn, so communication is so much richer when you use all the instruments at your disposal.

Spend time with each other. This is absolutely essential. You cannot have meaningful communication without it. If you are too busy to have time alone with each other, then you are too busy. You need to set your priorities and arrange your schedule accordingly.

One couple came to me with deep problems. As they shared their feelings with me it was immediately evident that their problem was a problem of communication. So I suggested that for fifteen minutes each night they sit down alone and simply talk with each other. I suggested a plan of action which they promised to follow. In the following week's session the tension was still high. I asked them if they had carried out the assignment I gave them. On only two nights did they spend time with each other. So I repeated the assignment. The next week they returned, the tension still high, the assignment still unfulfilled. We had only one further session, and they soon parted ways with each other. The tragedy is that they could have worked through their problems, for they were not that serious. And their marriage could have been saved. But they refused to take the time that was necessary.

Avoid foul play. Philip Yancey suggests several elements of foul play in marital communication, among them are the following:

1. Don't criticize your mate publicly.
2. Don't criticize things which cannot be changed.
3. Don't use physical violence.
4. Don't store up complaints and unload them at once.
5. Don't threaten divorce.
6. Don't generalize with "you always . . . ." Be specific.
7. Don't fight to determine a winner or loser. Seek mutual satisfaction.

These foul play tactics are out of bounds for communication in marriage.[10]

Practice. There is no substitute for practice. If the lines of communication are blocked, you can get them open again. If the communication in your marriage is good, it can be better. Communication is the key to marriage. Dialogue is to your marriage what blood is to the body. Put these principles to work and experience the exhilarating difference.

The Program

Here are some positive steps you can take.

1. Begin praying together. This co-communication with God will help open the communication lines between you.

2. Make one night a week your D-night (dialogue night). When the children are in bed, turn the television off and spend at least thirty minutes talking with each other. Let husband and wife each take about fifteen min-

utes. While the other one talks, practice listening. Talk about nonvolatile subjects.

3. Try positive interaction. Begin to focus on the positive. Compliment your mate. Commend him/her when there is something to commend. If necessary, make a list and share it on your D-night.

4. Develop nonverbal skills. Answer the question "Even when you do not say it, I know you are_____ when you . . . ." Fill in the blank with happy, nervous, angry, preoccupied, sad, feeling sexy, or disappointed with me. Determine the appropriate response for each and then share these findings with each other.

5. Read. Communication is an area of importance in every field, and much resource material is available. Check your church or city library for sources.

6. Most important, stay after it. During the dark days of World War II, Winston Churchill was invited back to Harrow, the school where he was educated. The speech he gave that day may hold the record for brevity. This was his entire speech: "Never give in! Never give in! Never! Never! Never!" [11] That's good advice for a marriage. Never give in to the problems which threaten to block your communication. Never! Never! Never!

7

The Second Time Around

Boaz and Ruth
Ruth 1—4

"Love is lovelier, the second time around." So goes the song. But is it true? Is love lovelier the second time around, or is it even possible? That question needs an answer in our day, for the number who try marriage a second time has mushroomed. Today, about one marriage in three involves remarriage for at least one of the partners.

Remarriage can involve a widowed man and a widowed woman, a widowed man and a divorced woman, a widowed man and a single woman, a divorced man and a widowed woman, a divorced man and a divorced woman, a divorced man and a single woman, a single man and a widowed woman, or a single man and a divorced woman. So common has remarriage become that one woman, completing a form for a job, filled in the blank concerning marital status with the response "unremarried."

Marriage, it seems, is like a beseiged fortress. Many of those on the inside want out, while those on the outside want in. Never have so many people bailed out of marriage so often. Yet, figures show that three out of four divorcees marry again and remarriage is also prevalent among those who have lost their mates by death. The time lapse varies little between the two groups, two and seven-tenths years separating a divorce and remarriage and three and five-tenths years separating the death of a mate and remarriage.[1] Even Mel Krantzler, whose book *Creative Divorce* led people all over our country to believe that being single is all right, entered the ranks of the remarried. A year after he was quoted as saying he would never marry again, Krantzler shocked his followers with a new direction (and a new book). His theme now is "Learning to love again." For all of its problems, marriage continues to be popular. The paradox of it all was vividly expressed by a woman who declared, "All men are selfish, brutal, and inconsiderate, and I wish I could find one!"

What causes a person to try marriage the second time? A desire for companionship is probably the primal motive. The conclusion of God that "It is not good that the man should be alone" (Gen. 2:18, KJV) has been confirmed in the experience of the formerly married. In one study of remarried couples, three fourths of the men and two thirds of the women cited companionship as the major reason for their second marriage.

Love, of course, is also one of the major motivations. A certain quip suggests that life is one crazy thing after another, and love is two crazy things after each other! Although maturity has removed the illusions of the romantic veil, the appeal of one person for another is still an important part of the relationship between humans. Love, although of a deeper, more discerning, more realistic type, often moves a person toward remarriage.

Other motivations are evident as well. Some simply want the benefit that the mate provides, a husband to fix things around the house or a wife to keep house and cook. Financial reasons are often involved. Not only can two live more cheaply than one, but two incomes provide more resources. In some cases, a person's status or occupation may increase the desirability for a mate. In addition, neurotic compulsions of one kind or another can move a person toward remarriage.

71

We see some of these motives at work in the relationship of a famous couple of yesteryear who tried marriage the second time, and liked it. The story of Ruth and Boaz is discussed in one of the most intriguing books of the Bible, the book of Ruth.

Ruth had married a young Jew whose family moved to Moab to escape a difficult economic situation in Israel. We don't know how long she was married to Mahlon before he died. It is not clear whether Ruth and Mahlon had been married for ten years before he died, or whether she had been widowed for ten years (Ruth 1:4). In either case, when her mother-in-law, Naomi, decided to return to her home, Ruth chose to go with her. The book of Ruth tells how this young widow entered again into the world of the married and it provides some insights into remarriage today.

The Possibility

Is remarriage a viable option for the formerly married? The basic thrust of Ruth's story is an affirmative. Not only is remarriage possible, but it can be a very positive experience.

Rehearse in your mind the details of Ruth's relationship with Boaz. How strange that the marriage ever took place. The plan seems to have originated in the mind of Naomi, Ruth's mother-in-law (2:19-22). An attempt of a friend or relative to play matchmaker for a formerly married person is usually unsuccessful if not disastrous. Not so in this case. The plan unfolds without a hitch. Chapters 3 and 4 of the book of Ruth show how Ruth chased Boaz until he caught her!

There were so many unfavorable factors in their relationship. For one thing, Ruth was a foreigner. That Boaz even noticed her was surprising (2:10). He was evidently much older than she (3:10). In a sense, he was obligated to marry her as the next of kin (her redeemer), and the whole affair was hastily conceived and concluded. Nevertheless, the joy bells of marriage the second time around rang with the delightful sound of success for Ruth. This remarriage would be forever celebrated in Israel for out of their union, three generations hence, would come the greatest Hebrew of them all, King David.

The same joy which Ruth and Boaz experienced the second time around, many experience today. The National Opinion Research Center conducted three social surveys on marital happiness in 1973, 1974, and 1975. Based on this data, a researcher concluded that there was no substantial difference in reported marital happiness between the remarried and those who were still with their first mate.[2]

Jesse Bernard, who has written a book on remarriage, reached the same conclusion from his research. The percentage of happiness among the remarried widow, he says, "does not differ greatly from that of the average run of marriages" and "those who . . . remarry after divorce have almost as high a percentage of success in the second marriage as the rest of the population has in its first marriage."[3]

Love can be lovelier the second time around, or at least as lovely. What are the factors that lead to success in a remarriage? Walter McKain, who carefully studied one hundred older remarried couples, isolated four success factors. He found that widows and widowers who knew each other well usually had a successful marriage. Also, remarriage which had the approval of friends and relatives had a greater chance for success than one which did not. In addition, satisfactory adjustment to the role changes which accompany aging was an important factor. One other factor of importance was home ownership. Widows and widowers who owned a home, but did not live in it after remarriage, tended to have successful remarriages.[4]

While all of those conclusions are true, I believe it would be more accurate to say that the possibility of success in remarriage is determined by the degree to which the couple deals with the unique problems which remarriage presents.

The Problems

There are, of course, some problems associated with the lot of the formerly married. These were alluded to in the introduction to this chapter, and are the motives which lead a person to try marriage a second time. However, the experience of remarriage does not remove the problems but instead adds a whole new set of problems. The unique difficulties of remarriage can be grouped in three general categories.

Money heads the list. In remarriage, money replaces sex as the number one cause of marital conflict. Attaining a new family with "yours" and "my" children is not always a blessing. Sometimes it is a burden.

In a first marriage, especially among young adults, "the flow of money seems to get settled in the mysterious alchemy of weaving a web of life together." [5] In remarriage, the individuals are more established in their patterns and something more than "mysterious alchemy" is required. Each individual has a financial status. Each usually has a source of income. Each has a pattern of paying bills and making financial decisions. Each has financial obligations to meet. A scheme must be developed to amalgamate these two systems.

Money matters relating to the children can also be sticky. If the children are small, what about allowances? How much and at what age? Care must be taken not to show favoritism toward either his or her children.

When property is involved or a large financial estate, the money problems can intensify. Many children oppose the remarriage of their widowed or divorced parent for fear of receiving a smaller portion of the inheritance. Child support payments also add to the financial strain.

Another problem of remarriage centers on the *children*. Not all remarriages include children. The marriage of Ruth and Boaz did not. But most do. The attempt to blend together the families and establish new patterns of relating is at the heart of remarital difficulties.

It may be a problem of competition. An only child may suddenly acquire a new brother or sister with whom he/she must compete for attention and accolades.

Or, it could be a problem of favoritism. It is extremely difficult for a parent to feel the same affection initially for the child of his/her mate. This might be reflected in inconsistent patterns of discipline or in inequitable allocations of the family income.

Another potential problem in remarriages is *comparison* with the former mate. In the case of a divorce, the former mate is still present as a perpetual reminder of former experiences, some of which at least were enjoyable. In the case of the widow or widower, the tendency of the widowed spouse to idealize the deceased mate is the critical factor.

While conscious comparison is usually kept to a minimum, it lurks just beneath the surface in most remarriages. Little slips like calling your new spouse by the name of your former mate, alluding to experiences you once had with your first partner, cherishing mementos and even furniture that you had once picked out with your first mate—all of these are factors of comparison.

The second time around, success will be determined by how you deal with these problems. Can you develop a new scheme for your financial affairs in which both of you are comfortable? Can you provide the kind of loving environment in which all your children—his/hers and yours—can feel important? Can you be secure enough about your new venture in love that allusions to the past do not cause you to feel uncomfortable? If so, love can be lovelier, or at least as lovely, the second time around.

The Program

If remarriage is a possibility, how can you prepare for it? Ruth provides an excellent example of the kind of attitude and approach to living in the single state that will enhance the probability of remarriage. Notice what she did.

First, *Ruth avoided self-pity.* Self-pity abounded in Naomi. She bemoaned the fact that she was too old to have a husband and past the point of having any more children (1:11-12). She complained that the hand of the Lord had gone against her (v. 13). She even wanted to change her name to Mara to perpetually proclaim the bitterness of her circumstances (1:20). She concluded that the Lord had dealt bitterly with her, bringing her home empty whereas she had gone out full (v. 21). Naomi bathed in self-pity, but there is no hint of it in Ruth.

That self-pity is common among the formerly married is quite obvious and, to a degree, understandable. In a radio broadcast, Paul Harvey posed the question, "What, of all life's experiences, puts us under the greatest sustained strain?" His answer was "the death of a spouse." Do you know what the second most stressful experience is, according to this famed broadcaster? Divorce. Divorce and death of a mate—those are the two doorways that lead into the world of the formerly married. Quite often the trauma of either of these experiences will produce the perturbing question, "Why has this experience happened to me?" That leads to self-pity.

Ralph W. Neighbour, Jr., a creative Baptist pastor-missionary, suggests eight steps that a divorced person often passes through on the road to wholeness:

1. The "No! It's not true" stage
2. The "I'm going to try again" stage
3. The "My husband is a rat" stage
4. The "All men are rats" stage
5. The "How do I handle sex now?" stage
6. The "How do I handle my children?" stage.
7. The "When will I remarry?" stage and
8. The "Settling in" stage.[6]

It is only when a person comes to the final stage that the blight of self-pity is defeated and the journey toward wholeness is possible.

Granger Westberg, in his book *Good Grief,* traces the similar stages that a person goes through in the process of grief:

1. The state of shock
2. Emotional reaction
3. Depression and loneliness
4. Physical symptoms of distress
5. Panic
6. Guilt about the loss
7. Resentment
8. Inability to return to normal activities
9. The gradual return of hope
10. Readjustment to reality [7]

Although we are not given any information about the way Ruth worked through her grief, we are shown where she ended up. Self-pity was gone, the bitterness had been dissolved, and a healthy acceptance of her situation had been established. Without this, the possibility of a successful remarriage is unlikely.

There is a second factor which Ruth reveals: *she took good care of herself.* She was careful to keep herself as appealing as she could. Notice chapter 2 of the book of Ruth. Boaz came to his field to check with his workers. Look at verse 5. A loose translation of this verse would be, "Wow! Who is that girl?" There was something about Ruth that made her stand out. She caught the eye of Boaz. Was it her physical beauty? Perhaps. More likely, it was a beauty of character that caused her to outshine the other workers.

The word *Ruth* is a contraction of the Hebrew word *reuth.* This Hebrew word might come from the root that means "the act of seeing" or sight," or "something worth seeing." In this case, Ruth's name could be a reference to her beauty. There is another root from which the Hebrew word might come. This root means friendship. In this case, Ruth's name could refer to her amiable and affectionate disposition.[8] I prefer to go with the latter idea. The beauty cult and *Playboy* philosophy notwithstanding, real beauty is not in the physical arrangement of a person's molecules but in the attitude or spirit which emanates from his/her character.

Some of the most attractive people I know are not pretty or handsome. They have been careful to develop their character while at the same time making themselves physically attractive. That's the second key which will lead to a successful remarriage. When you lose your spouse, by death or divorce, don't let yourself go. Take care of yourself. Be neat and clean. Keep yourself in good physical shape. Most of all, be the kind of person that others enjoy being around. There is a ring of truth in the evaluation made by Dr. Robert Burns, a former minister. He suggested that at twenty a woman has the face God gave her. At thirty she has a face made possible by cosmetics. At forty her face displays the skill of her hairdresser and masseuse. Her face at fifty reflects the way her husband treats her. But at sixty she has the face she gave herself.[9]

There is another element in the story of Ruth, perhaps the most important of all: *Ruth stayed involved in life.* There is a tendency to withdraw from people when you go through the trauma of divorce or death. To drop out of life seems, at times, to be the easiest way out. Notice, however, in Ruth this tendency was thwarted.

In chapter 1, Ruth refused to leave Naomi. The oration of Ruth in verses 16 and 17 is perhaps the most moving in all the Bible. Was it the spirit of adventure or her allegiance to Naomi's God which prompted this response? We cannot tell for sure. In either case, it is clear that Ruth refused to drop out of life. She was ready to move into the future.

Then look what Ruth does in chapter 2. She knows that food has to be found so that she and Naomi can eat. So immediately she pursues the only course available: she goes to glean in the fields. A time-honored tradition in Israel was to leave some of the crops unharvested for the poor and the widows. Ruth took advantage of this tradition. We see that it was in the daily duties of carrying out her work that she met the man who was to be her future husband.

Many of the formerly married ask me, "Where can I meet an eligible man or woman?" That's not an easy question to answer. But I am sure of this much. You will never meet a person who might possibly be a remarriage partner for you if you check out of life. Go to work. Get involved in a church with a single's group. We have had numerous marriages which have come out of the single adult group in our church. Take advantage of the legitimate services for the formerly married in your city. Play tennis. Get on a ball team. Join a ceramics class.

Become part of a bowling league. Get involved in life! Quite often you will discover, as Ruth did, that in the daily activities of living, your path will cross with the man or woman who is right for you to join in a new venture in the world of the married.

Conclusion

A preacher said to one of the older single adults in his church, "I heard you are getting married." "It's not true," the lady answered, "but thanks for the rumor."

There are some who are not thankful for the rumor, for they are happily single. Because of their goals in life they would not welcome married life. But for those who desire the married life again, the good news is that it can be as lovely the second time around, despite the accompanying problems. To prepare yourself for the possibility, remember these three keys:

1. Avoid self-pity.
2. Take care of yourself.
3. Stay involved in life.

8

In-laws or Outlaws?

David and Michal
1 Samuel 18-19

As two young husbands discussed their marriages, one said to the other, "My mother-in-law has a problem. She has an interferiority complex!"

If there was ever an in-law with an interferiority complex it was King Saul, father of Michal and father-in-law of David. The story of David and Michal's relationship is a sad tale of marriage commenced at the altar of mutual concern but eventually shattered on the crucible of mutual contempt. A quick perusal of the story of their rocky relationship will reveal that an in-law problem was the key to their mutual discord. Saul agreed to the marriage in the first place because he felt Michal would somehow detract David from his military success (1 Sam. 18:21). Saul's conniving is evident in the dowry he demanded of David (v. 25), but his plan failed. Saul then attempted to kill David, forcing Michal to choose between her father and her husband (1 Sam. 19:11-12). Saul simply would not leave them alone.

The problem is still with us today. Judson and Mary Landis reported on a study of marital problems in which in-law problems were ranked as the second most serious marital difficulty by the women. The men ranked it third. In another study of 544 university couples in early marriage, problems with in-laws were ranked number one.[1]

The mobility of our day, which makes it less likely

that a couple will live in the same community as their in-laws, does alleviate some of the tension. The problem, however, is not merely a matter of geography. The deeper emotional and psychological ties still provide the raw material out of which in-law problems can develop. So the problem is still with us.

And the problem is universal. When George Murdock did a cross-cultural survey of two hundred and fifty societies around the world, he discovered that 81 percent of the societies had some form of mother-in-law difficulty.[2]

Although the difficulty can stem from any of the in-law relationships, it has been indisputably certified that the mother-in-law is the prime figure in in-law disputes. Why? Perhaps because the family has traditionally been the woman's domain. Emotionally, a mother's tie with her children is probably deeper. This has led to a preponderance of mother-in-law jokes which portray the typical mother-in-law as one who talks too much, knows all the answers, is a meddlesome troublemaker, is ego deflating, is mean, is a loathsome object of aggression, comes too often and stays too long, and is best dealt with at a distance. My favorite mother-in-law joke is about the mother-in-law who was so nearsighted that she nagged a coathanger for an hour before she realized it was not her son-in-law.

With such jokes typical of our understanding, it needs to be decisively declared that all in-laws in general and all mothers-in-law in particular are not bad. In the Bible there are the stories of Jethro, the wise and understanding father-in-law of Moses (Ex. 18), and Naomi, the supportive and helpful mother-in-law of Ruth (Ruth). These can be paralleled by many of you who experience positive, warm relationships with your in-laws.

At the same time, it is clear that many in-laws are not of the positive variety. Numerous marriages that have gone on the rocks today have done so because of insuperable ill-treatment by in-laws.

There are two periods when the problems with in-laws become major factors in a marriage: in the early years when the young couple is seeking to become independent, and in the latter years when the parents are becoming dependent. It was in the former period that the in-law difficulty of David and Michal was at its height. A closer look at their experience will help us to understand some of the reasons for in-law tension today.

Why In-law Problems?

Why is there so often tension in the relationship between in-laws? What are the roots of the problem? I heard of a Chinese bride who left her husband because her mother-in-law slept under their bed! That is, of course, an extreme example. Evelyn Duvall in her classic book on the subject, *In-Laws: Pro and Con,* gives the results of her extensive studies in this area of family life. She lists fifteen reasons most often cited as the cause of problems with a mother-in-law. A mother-in-law is problematic because she: (1) meddles; (2) is possessive; (3) nags and complains; (4) is indifferent; (5) is immature; (6) is old-fashioned; (7) is inconsistent; (8) plays favorites; (9) abuses hospitality; (10) is self-righteous; (11) talks too much; (12) is deceitful; (13) covets what the children have; (14) does not take care of her own home; and (15) drinks or gambles.[3] With a little adjustment most of these could be applied to the other in-laws.

I think these causes can be summarized into four general categories, most of which appear in the tumultuous triangle of David, Michal, and Saul.

The first reason for in-law trouble is *hatred*. That is, many parents simply do not like their prospective son- or daughter-in-law.

This is very evident in our text. Saul did not like David. Verse 9 says that Saul looked at David with suspicion. Verses 10-11 show that Saul tried to kill David. Verse 15 indicates that Saul dreaded David. Verse 29 reveals that Saul was David's enemy continually. Saul did not like David. He had a personal hatred for David that led him to constantly interfere in the relationship between David and Michal.

This dislike, which is at the heart of most in-law problems today, is caused by several factors.

Most parents do not think the prospective in-law is good enough to be married to their child. The suitor lacks the maturity or the ability or the looks or the promise that their child deserves. Their child could do better. One suitor told his girlfriend, "If you don't marry me, I'll blow my brains out." She laughed and said, "That would be a joke on Daddy. He doesn't think you have any." The oldest of our four children is only eight, but I can already identify with this feeling. I can't imagine anyone being qualified to marry my daughter!

Sometimes the prospective in-law is of a lower social level than their child. This idea appears in our text as David remonstrated that neither on personal grounds nor on account of his social standing nor because of his lineage did he deserve to be the king's son-in-law (1 Sam. 18:18,23). I'm sure that Saul agreed. The fact that marriages between people of different social levels sometimes creates additional problems has already been dealt with in chapter three.

Sometimes it is jealousy that causes the hatred. This jealousy might take the form of a mother who cannot stand to think of anyone else providing for her "baby." Or the jealousy might come out of competition between the father-in-law and son-in-law. Such was the case between Saul and David. It was after the women of Israel sang, "Saul has slain his thousands, and David his ten thousands" (v. 7), that the Bible says Saul looked at David with suspicion.

Or it can happen as a result of incompatible personalities. There are some people who simply cannot stand being around each other because of some personal quirk that one or both of them has. The daughter's dreamboat may be repulsive to Mother and obnoxious to Daddy! Many times a personal antipathy toward the son-in-law or daughter-in-law is at the root of the problem.

A second reason for in-law problems is *habit*. After being the primary resource person for your child for at least eighteen years, it is extremely difficult to let go of the reins immediately and completely.

John Drakeford talks about an "emotional umbilical cord" which he asserts is more difficult to sever than the physical one.[4] This is usually more evident in the mother-in-law than in the father-in-law, especially if the mother-in-law does not work outside the home. In that case, her significance has been largely rooted in the lives of the children. Because there is no suitable substitute to take the place of the children, she will be hesitant to let them go. The pains of a mother trying to deliver a child after adolescence are often as severe as the ones that she experienced in giving birth to the child.

Giving advice to our children, protecting them, and providing for them have been lifelong habits. The difficulty of breaking such habits is often a source of in-law discord.

A third reason for in-law problems is *help*. That is, much of the trouble which parents-in-law cause is simply the result of their desire to help provide for the struggling newlyweds a better life than what they themselves experienced.

It is, of course, the American ideal for children, when

they get married, to be totally independent. Margaret Mead has pointed out that few human societies have encouraged young people to start a new family with such small backing from parents and kinship groups.[5]

Recent social trends, however, like the tendency of couples to marry young while still in school, are countering this independent ideal and ushering in an era of more dependence. It is more common today for parents to subsidize education than it was ten years ago. This parental subsidy can be helpful in many ways, but it can also precipitate numerous problems.

One lady suggests a testing device called an "in-law antenna" which an interested, well-meaning mother- or father-in-law could send up to test the atmosphere when in doubt about something they want to do for their children-in-law.[6] Until such a device is invented, in-law problems will continue to come from many well-meaning parents-in-law who are just trying to help.

A fourth reason for in-law problems is *hurt*. We often criticize our in-laws. But they are human, too. And they can be hurt. When Saul discovered how Michal had deceived him he cried out, not in anger but in hurt, "Why have you deceived me like this and let my enemy go?" (19:17). Many parents-in-law look at their children with the same kind of hurt as they cry out, "Why do you treat us like you do?"

Evelyn Duvall's study shows that the two top-ranking criticisms that parents-in-law have of children-in-law is that they are indifferent and thoughtless.[7] Said one mother-in-law, "Anything I do is wrong. If I leave them alone, they accuse me of being neglectful. If I spend time with them, they accuse me of imposing. If I appear interested in them, they accuse me of meddling. If I do not appear interested in them, they accuse me of indifference. I just can't win."

Mothers-in-law and fathers-in-law are first of all people with feelings. When they are neglected and not accepted, when they are manipulated and used, when the other set of parents receive more attention, they are hurt. And that hurt can lead to problems.

What Can Be Done?

Hatred, habit, help, and hurt—under those four categories most in-law problems can be categorized. What then can we do about them?

There must be *a proper start.* An old Jewish proverb states, "When a child gets married, he divorces his mother." This does not mean that the child no longer cares about his/her parents. Nor does it suggest that these parent-child relationships do not exist. They do. Every married person is a member of three families: mine, yours, and ours. What it does mean is that from the beginning the husband-wife relationship must be put in the primary category.

This is why the leaving and cleaving process of Genesis 2:24 is so important. The Bible describes marriage in these words, "For this cause a man shall leave his father and his mother, and shall cleave to his wife; and they shall become one flesh."

The word *leave (azab)* literally means to abandon or to forsake. It is the same word used in Genesis 39:12 when the Bible says that Potiphar's wife caught hold of Joseph's garment and begged him to go to bed with her. "But he left his garment in her hand, and fled and got out of the house" (RSV). It implies a permanent and deliberate setting aside. Because of what the Bible says about our responsibility to care for our parents, we cannot interpret this verse to mean a total separation from our parents. But it does definitely mean that we must effectively separate ourselves from our parents.

The word *cleave (dabaq)* literally means to adhere to or be glued to. It implies the closest kind of bond, a bond that is inseparable and permanent.

I stress this leaving and cleaving process in every wedding I perform. I point out that a wedding is a time of realignment in our relationships. The young man and woman are beginning a new relationship which is to take priority over every other human relationship. I clarify this fact and ask the parents if they will accept their children in the new secondary relationship to them. This does not, of course, settle the matter. At least it does verbalize it.

If from the beginning of our marriage we will effectively break our ties with our parents and unreservedly commit ourselves to our mates, and if our parents will accept this change, many in-law problems will be avoided.

Then there must be a *proper stance*. A proper start will not automatically eliminate all the problems. It only lays the foundation. Problems will continue to arise. Thus, a proper stance is necessary to deal with these continuing problems.

What is the proper stance? Togetherness. Always stand together as a husband and wife. Never let the immaturity or the interference of in-laws dissolve that basic commitment to each other.

One man concludes that most in-law problems revolve around two basic issues, the primary of which is value judgment. That is, the inability or unwillingness on the part of each spouse to rank in order whom they value the most: relatives, parents, or spouse. He asserts that it is almost impossible for in-law problems to arise when the husband and wife always value their spouse the highest.[8]

Begin with a recognition that your primary relationship is to each other. Express that conviction to your parents, and then honor that commitment at each point along the way. Face each decision from this perspective, "How will this affect our relationship as husband and wife."

Once that pattern is established you will be free to take the third step which is *proper stroking*. Every person needs some stroking sometimes, and parents-in-law are persons. Evelyn Duvall discovered in her study that a mother-in-law today tends to feel unimportant, unwanted, and uncared for.[9] They need to feel wanted. They want to feel accepted. They need some stroking.

At the heart of God's commandments to his people is the challenge to "Honor your father and your mother" (Ex. 20:12). The word *honor* implies more than respect. It also means to provide for. Nothing I have said is meant to detract from that basic command of God. Someone has pointed out the irony of the fact that a couple can care for several children growing up, but several children often fail to care for one set of parents growing old!

Sometimes the best defense is a good offense. Shower your in-laws with love and you may discover that many of your problems will dissolve in the context of warmth and appreciation.

Then there needs to be *proper scheduling*. You need to arrange your schedule to find some time with your families. This needs to include holidays as well as surprise times. Early in your marriage you should discuss the meaning of holidays for each family and in light of that discussion, make plans on the most acceptable way of arranging your schedule. Time together will often be the way of cementing a relationship with in-laws and helping it to mature.

What about from the perspective of the parents-in-law? What can they do to avoid in-law irritations?

The first step is *acceptance*. If your child has made the decision to marry, your refusal to accept the prospective mate will do one of two things. It will add extra tension to their relationship thus decreasing the chance of their making it, or, it will sever your relationship with your child.

Besides, sometimes you may be less than honest in your evaluation of your child. Your opinion that your son or daughter could have done better might be based more on personal attachment than on fact. It is impossible for parents to be completely objective in the evaluation of their child and the prospective mate. So the best approach is to accept the in-law and expect the best. Sometimes your attitude of acceptance can be self-fulfilling.

Another important factor is *affection.* Often parents will continue to show favoritism to their son or daughter to the exclusion of the in-law. Such favoritism will convey to the in-law that, whatever you have said, you really do not accept him/her. On special occasions, like Christmas and birthdays, my mother-in-law always shows as much or more affection to me as to her daughter. She is a smart lady, for she is creating an environment in which healthy in-law relationships can grow.

Conclusion

Saul was a father-in-law with an interferiority complex. As a result, the marriage of David and Michal was adversely affected. In their case the word *in-laws* was synonymous with "outlaws." But it does not have to be that way. By following the above suggestions your relationship with in-laws can be a rich and rewarding experience.

9

In the Worst of Times

Nabal and Abigail
1 Samuel 25

"I take you to be my wife, to have and to hold, from this day forward, for better or for worse . . . ." When we repeat those words at our wedding, we do not really expect the worst to happen. We anticipate good times together and look forward to the best that the marriage experience has to offer. We consider the statistics which convey widespread marital unhappiness as irrelevant. We are convinced that what is happening to so many around us simply will not happen to us.

Probably Abigail felt the same way on her wedding night. Abigail was a young woman who was a combination of brains and beauty. She was "of good understanding" (v.3, KJV), the Bible says, "and of a beautiful countenance." There is continuing debate about whether men find beauty or intelligence more appealing in a woman, with equally vocal supporters lined up on each side. The point of the biblical description of Abigail is to inform us that she had both! What a catch she was.

Now focus on Nabal, the man she was to marry. He gives all appearances of being the most eligible bachelor in town. The Bible says that Nabal was very great, which means great in possessions and money. That is, he was rich. He was also well-established in his business, wise in the ways of the world. Here was a man Abigail thought would provide her security, affection, and contentment. As she said "I do" and claimed this man for her husband, what joyful expectations she had.

Soon, however, those starry-eyed dreams began to crumble as she woke up to the reality of the person whom she had married. The Bible says that Nabal was "churlish" (v. 3, KJV), which means rude or cruel. He was selfish, refusing to share what he had with others (v. 11). He was an alcoholic, and his drinking only intensified the other unpleasant elements of his character (v. 36). He is described as a son of Belial which denotes both the excesses of his moral life and the emptiness of his spiritual life (v. 17, KJV). That he was not a believer is evident from his life. In addition to all of that, Nabal was a fool (v. 25).

The man Abigail took for better or for worse was much worse than she thought! Instead of the best of times, her marriage turned out to be the worst of times.

There are many today who can identify with Abigail's plight. You, too, began marriage with bright expectations for a fulfilling life. But the longer you are with your mate the more you are aware of those traits and behavior patterns that were reflected in Nabal.

Self-centeredness or stinginess is certainly a problem in many marriages today. Living in the "me decade," many homes are plagued with individuals who insist on doing it "my way." I believe selfishness is at least a contributing factor in every instance of marital discord.

Cruelty that manifests itself in mental or physical abuse is becoming more common. Abigail Van Buren of "Dear Abby" fame said that a man who beats a woman is sick. And any woman who sticks around for repeated beatings is sicker. If that's true, there are a growing number of sick people in marriages. One study suggests that as many as 4.5 million American women have been battered at least once by the men they think they love. Chicago police estimate that over 25 percent of the city's aggravated assaults, where the victim ends up in the hospital, are women abused by husbands or boyfriends. Wife-beating is perhaps "one of this country's least recognized and most appalling social problems." [1] Nabal was not alone in his churlishness.

The fact that drinking causes problems in the home is incontestable. Eighteen percent of the homes in America are troubled by a problem drinker. Ann Landers concludes that alcohol had ruined more marriages than anything else known to man. The appealing challenge to grab for all the gusto you can, issued by beautiful people, does not pull back the curtain to reveal the havoc which uncontrolled drinking produces in the home.

The difficulty experienced when a believer and a nonbeliever are linked together in the most intimate of relationships is a reality with many of you. Paul's admonition, "Do not be bound together with unbelievers" (2 Cor. 6:14), was given for a reason. To defy it is to invite problems.

The foolishness of the acts and attitudes of ourselves and our mates is everywhere evident. One couple was at a party. The husband was telling a story about something that happened the night before. "We were sitting in the living room," he said, "and a mouse ran across the room . . ." His wife interrupted him, "No, it was a rat." "It was a mouse," he countered. With rising anger she returned, "No, it was a rat." They became so angry that he ended up sleeping in a motel by himself that night. Realizing how foolish he had been, he went back home the next morning and apologized. "I'm sorry," he told his wife. "How foolish to separate over a story about a stupid mouse." "It was a rat," she said. And there they went again! How foolish we often are in our actions and reactions.

The point is that everything Abigail had to face in

Nabal is still with us today in one form or another. There are many who have walked down the aisle with the best of intentions and the richest expectations who have instead discovered their marriages to be humiliating, hurt-evoking experiences. Instead of good times they experience bad times. When the worst comes, what can you do?

You Can Do the Worst of Things

When you find yourself in a situation like that of Abigail, that is, when the worst comes in your marriage, you can do the worst of things. You can react negatively. There are several negative reactions which Abigail could have made and which often are made today. These are options that are open to you.

The first of these is *retaliation*. When you are in a marriage where your mate makes life miserable for you, then you can retaliate by making life miserable for him/her. "An eye for an eye, a tooth for a tooth" is not merely some relic of ancient Hebrew ethics. It is a standard operating procedure in many marriages today.

Obviously, the marriage relationship generates more anger than any other situation. The dynamics of marriage makes such friction inevitable. It is not the anger itself, but how we deal with the anger that is the problem. Rather than diffusing it through communication and forgiveness, we often handle it negatively.

One lady went to a marriage counselor. She carried an 8½ by 11-inch notebook, over an inch thick. She explained that this was her record of all the wrong things her husband had ever done. It's no wonder her husband described her as a one-woman grievance committee always in session. She kept a flame going under her anger so that at any moment it could explode into open retaliation.

It is common for husbands and wives to react to their mates with anger and bitterness. The folly of this approach, however, is that the individual hurts himself more by his anger than he hurts his mate. Victor Hugo said it like this, "Pride robs me of God, envy of my neighbor, anger of myself." [2]

Retaliation is an option when the worst comes, but we see no hint of it in Abigail.

Another negative response is *withdrawal*. There are two ways of striking back: by blowing up and by clamming up. Sometimes the latter is the most devastating. Everyone has tried his hand at the silent treatment enough to know how utterly frustrated it will make your mate. If you want to make your mate mad, just ignore her. When she walks in the room, act like she is not there. When she asks a question, don't answer. Just ignore her. It will drive her up the wall.

There are those who respond to their unpleasant circumstances by withdrawing into their own little world, refusing to talk, and sinking down into a good old sulk. That word *sulk* is an interesting word. A sulky is defined in the dictionary as "a light two-wheeled vehicle accommodating one person." From that noun and adjective has been derived the word *sulk* which means sullenly aloof, withdrawn, self-isolated. [3]

What a description of the atmosphere of many homes! The togetherness is gone. Rather than a one-flesh relationship there are two individuals isolated in their own little worlds. A quick glance at our text, however, will show that this was not the approach Abigail took.

A third negative response is *infidelity*. That is, if things are bad at home, get your kicks somewhere else.

Statistics indicate that in 50 percent of all marriages today either the husband or the wife has committed adultery at least once. What the statistics do not show is that more often than not the infidelity is a *result* of a marriage breakdown rather than the *cause* of the breakdown. It is an attempt to gain satisfaction which is lacking at home.

The story in our text, however, repeatedly implies the faithfulness of Abigail to her husband. Infidelity was not an out for her.

Another negative alternative is *divorce*. When the worst of times comes, you can just check it in. When the flame goes out, you can go find another match to light.

It seems like we have come full circle on this matter in the last twenty years. Twenty years ago, even when your marriage relationship became strained, there was strong pressure against a divorce. You just tried to work it out. Today, when your marriage relationship becomes strained in the least, there is a strong pressure to get a divorce. Trying to work it out used to be the only alternative. It is fast becoming the last alternative. Divorce has taken its place as the primary out when the worst comes.

I do not deny that as a last resort, divorce is sometimes the only alternative left. Nor do I condemn those who are divorced. I just believe that many marriages which actually could be salvaged are wrecked on the rocks of too quick and too easy divorce.

Divorce itself is not without problems. There is the inevitable loneliness. This is what I hear most often. "I can make it all right through the day," one lady recently told me, "but the nights are unbearable." A certain frustration also accompanies divorce. This frustration might be expressed in guilt ("I can't do anything right") or in self-pity ("Everything always goes wrong for me!"). When a divorcee works through the immediate bitterness and is ready to seek companionship from the other sex, she is usually shocked by the pressures and expectations that are part of the dating game today. The sexual pressures are almost overwhelming. When children are involved, the divorcee has to adjust to the new role as single parent as well.

What Elton Trueblood said about the intellectual dimension of life also applies to the relational. He suggests that it is not wise to give up a position when it seems to involve difficulties, unless it is possible to find an alternative position that exhibits less serious difficulties.[4] Before you escape from a marriage with problems by the avenue of divorce, you need to carefully consider which alternative is beset with more difficulties.

Sometimes the worst will come in your marriage. When it does, you can do the worst of things. You can retaliate, you can withdraw, you can try infidelity, you can succumb to the pressure for a hasty divorce. You can react negatively.

You Can Do the Best of Things

We see, however, that Abigail did not opt for any of those alternatives. Instead, she tried the positive approach. Somewhere in England there is a tombstone on which are etched the words, "In the worst of times, he did the best of things." What an epitaph! And what a beautiful description of Abigail, for this phrase accurately portrays her approach to her problems.

In the worst of times Abigail did the best of things—*she devoted herself to her husband*. Rather than retaliate toward him or withdraw from him, she did everything she could to help him.

Someone has said that a perfect wife is one who doesn't expect a perfect husband. (The opposite is true, too.) Abigail was a perfect wife in that sense for she recognized the faults of her husband but loved him anyway. Her love was not of the "because" variety but of the "in spite of" variety. She did not fight fire with fire. Rather, she tried to put it out with kindness.

We often compare marriage to a contract we make to buy a car or a home. However, Christian marriage differs from an ordinary contract in a significant way. Contracts are "if . . . then" agreements. If you do this, then I will respond with this. A failure on the part of either of the parties to fulfill the obligations of the contract will invalidate it. In a Christian marriage there is no place for the word *if.* You do not say to the bride "If you will stay young, if you will remain beautiful, if you will always be loving, then I take you to be my wife." No! By saying the words "for better or for worse, for richer or for poorer, in health and in sickness" you accept the possibility that the bad times will come, but you give the assurance that even if they do, you will stay together. If, instead of looking for a way out, you look for a way to make things better, you may not want out.

Cecil Osborne tells of a woman who told her marriage counselor she hated her husband. She not only wanted to divorce him, she wanted to make his life miserable. The marriage counselor said, "Here is a plan. Shower your husband with compliments, overwhelm him with kindness, indulge his every whim. Make him realize how much he needs you—then start divorce proceedings. It will wipe him out." She decided to try the plan. Six months later she saw her counselor. He asked if she were ready to divorce her husband. "Oh, no," she said, "I followed your advice and we've never been happier. I love him with all my heart." [5]

If your marriage is not what it ought to be, someone has to take the initiative to try to make it better. That is what Abigail did. And so can you. When your marriage experiences the worst of times, do the best of things—

devote yourself to your husband, devote yourself to your wife, smother your mate with kindness and affection, and see the difference it makes.

In the worst of times Abigail did the best of things—*she developed her own individuality.* Read the story again and you will be almost overwhelmed by the charm, the cleverness, and the confidence that Abigail exhibited.

Granted that Abigail didn't have the best of circumstances. The point is that she did not let her unpleasant circumstances deter her personal development nor did she allow the churlishness of her husband to destroy her own charm and grace. Rather, she used the unpleasant circumstances of her marriage as the caldron in which she developed, purified, and polished the strengths of her own personality. We are not always responsible for the circumstances of our lives, but we are responsible for how we react to those circumstances. Abigail realized that, so she assumed responsibility for her own life and sought to realize the potential God had planted within her.

Alfred Adler tells a story about two men who bumped into each other at a railway station in Austria one day. One of the men, an alcoholic, begged of the other man enough money to buy one more bottle of wine. The other responded with surprise that such an intelligent-looking man could sink to the status of living from one drink to another. The beggar explained that the cards of life had been stacked against him. His mother died when he was young. His father had beaten him and his brothers and sisters unmercifully. Then, when World War I came, the family was permanently separated. "You see," he said, "I never had a chance."

The other man responded, "This is very strange for my background is similar to yours. I, too, lost my mother when I was young. My father was also brutal, and the war separated me from my family as well. I felt that I had no choice but to try to overcome these circumstances rather than to be overcome by them." As the two men continued to talk they made an incredible discovery—they were blood brothers, long separated from the trauma of war! [6]

Here were two individuals who came out of similar circumstances but who ended up at a different destination. Why? Because of the way they chose to respond to the events of their lives.

In the worst of times Abigail did the best of things—*she deepened her faith in God.*

It is always difficult to faithfully devote your life to God. When you are living with a man or woman who does not share your spiritual concern, it is even more difficult. Yet, it is not impossible. It can be done.

Nabal evidently did not share his wife's faith. Nevertheless, not in a pious, obnoxious way, but in a consistent, caring way Abigail followed the personal disciplines that enabled her spiritual life to grow and her relationship with God to develop. In unpleasant circumstances she did what was necessary to deepen her faith in God. In the long run, it is more important to be rightly related to God than it is to be rightly related to your mate.

Conclusion

Cecil Osborne has said that there is a universal law of mind and spirit that applies to the family and can be divided into three parts: (1) I can change no other person by direct action; (2) I can change only myself; (3) when I change, others tend to change in reaction to me. [7] Long before Dr. Osborne stated that law, Abigail exhibited it. In the worst of times, she did the best of things.

10

When Sex Goes Haywire

David and Bathsheba
2 Samuel 11:1 to 12:20

The marriage of dynamic David and beautiful Bathsheba was established on the foundation of lust. It was sex, not love, that brought these two together. This marriage of a Hebrew monarch to the wife of one of his leading warriors is an insightful illustration of what happens when sex goes haywire.

The story of David and Bathsheba reminds us that the control of our sexual desire is no new problem. Some people seem to think that we have invented sex today. Actually, the sexual dimension has been a part of human nature ever since God created man out of the dust of the earth, breathed life into his nostrils, and planted man and woman in the garden.

Of course, the church's evaluation of sex has not always been the same. In each century the church's view has been influenced by the culture in which it existed. Thus, many of the early church fathers, touched by the dualism of their Greek culture, had negative views of sex. Martin Luther once expressed his puzzlement over the complexity of sex: "Had God consulted me in the matter, I should have advised him to continue the generation of the species by fashioning the human beings out of clay as Adam was made." In the age of Victorian prudery, sex was such a taboo subject that the legs of pianos were covered to prevent suggestiveness, pregnancy was called an "interesting condition," and the sexual dimension of life was never discussed in mixed company.[1]

This negative approach to sex, and the reticence in discussing it, are not found in the Bible. The Bible not only talks about sex, but also provides a very positive, healthy view of sex. The person who referred to the three D's of sex as duty, dull, and dirty was not talking about the teaching of God's Word.[2] The biblical view of sex is positive.

The Bible declares that *sex is God's idea*. Genesis 1:27 says that God created man as male and female. Immediately after he created Adam and Eve with this sexual propensity, God told them to be fruitful and multiply and replenish the earth. Notice that this was before the fall. Sex is not a result of the fall. It is part of God's original plan. God made us the way we are. Sex is God's idea.

In addition, the Bible proposes that *sex is good*. In Genesis 1:31, the Bible says, "And God saw all that He had made [and that includes man and woman in their sexual dimension], and behold, it was very good." The picturesque expressions in Proverbs 5:18-19 reemphasize the positive value of sex with the implication that sex is to be enjoyed by a husband and wife. The Song of Solomon is even more explicit. Some have tried to allegorize the Song of Solomon. They say that it is an explanation in figurative language of God's love for man. That may be, but behind the figurative analogy is the factual proclamation of the beauty and pleasure and goodness of this sexual propensity of human life with which God has endowed us.

Then, the Bible also declares that *the arena for the expression of this sexual dimension is marriage*. In Matthew 19:5, when Jesus makes reference to God's ideal purpose for man in marriage by quoting Genesis 2:24, "FOR THIS CAUSE A MAN SHALL LEAVE HIS

102

FATHER AND MOTHER, AND SHALL CLEAVE TO HIS WIFE; AND THE TWO SHALL BECOME ONE FLESH," he was saying that sex is for marriage. In 1 Corinthians 7:2-5 Paul states that one of the reasons for marriage is to enable the partners to fulfill each other's sexual needs.

The sexual dimension in human life is to provide new life, to unite two people in body and spirit, and to provide the opportunity to communicate in an intimate way with another person. God intended all of this to happen in the security, sanctity, and sensitivity of a permanent marriage relationship. This means, as one person has put it, "Sex is therefore not to be despised, nor disregarded, nor defiled, nor deified, but is to be reverently accepted as a gift of God to be received with thanksgiving, and enjoyed, and used for his glory." [3]

Sex and marriage go together. Marriage is to provide for the expression of our sexual selves, and sex is to be a vital part of marriage. There are, of course, times when for good reason husbands and wives must set aside their physical needs. David Mace concludes, however, that the neglect of sex in marriage leads to danger and sometimes to disaster.[4] The sexual relationship is not to be neglected. It is an important part of your marriage. You nourish this dimension of your marriage when you provide the right atmosphere, take proper care of your body, and are sensitive to the differences between you and your mate.

There is a fourth factor that the Bible affirms about sex: *sex is not to be abused.* When it is experienced at the right time, in the right place, between the right people, for the right reasons, sex is one of the most productive forces of life. When it is misused and abused, it becomes one of life's most destructive forces.

This is what we see in the relationship of David and

103

Bathsheba. Look at the experience described in 2 Samuel 11. Sexual desire was the initiating motive of their relationship. David saw Bathsheba; he desired her; he sent for her; and he slept with her. It is a story that has sex written all over it. Unfortunately, it was sex at the wrong time, in the wrong place, with the wrong person, for the wrong reason. David and Bathsheba let sex get out of hand!

In a day when that tragedy is oft repeated, whether it is by two teenagers in the back seat of a parked car or by an unsatisfied husband or wife seeking thrills in an extramarital relationship, this story provides some clear answers to the disturbing question: what happens when sex gets out of hand?

It Brings Displeasure of God

The narrative of David and Bathsheba's relationship in chapter 11 ends with this succinct statement: "But the thing that David had done displeased the Lord" (v. 27, KJV). In 1 Kings 15:5 David's glorious reign as king of Israel was summarized in these words: "David did that which was right in the eyes of the Lord, and turned not aside from any thing that he commanded him all the days of his life, save only in the matter of Uriah the Hittite" (KJV).

Do you hear what the Bible says? God did not like what David and Bathsheba did. The death of the baby conceived in this promiscuous meeting, the disturbing accusation of the prophet Nathan, the disappearance from David's life of the joy of his salvation, and the disruptions in his family life—all these elements in the story simply reinforce the fact of God's displeasure. God created sex for a purpose, you see, and he provided a place for it to be experienced. Whenever we deviate from God's plan, God is displeased.

104

This is not the popular philosophy of our day, of course. The prophets of the new morality proclaim the liberation of modern man to do what he wants to do. The playboy philosophers say that there are to be no limitations on sex. The crowd says join in the fun. Do what makes you feel good. It's OK. But the Bible says (and David and Bathsheba's experience illustrates it) that when sex gets out of hand, whether it is before marriage or outside of marriage, it brings the displeasure of God.

It Brings Difficulties

In 2 Samuel 12, Nathan, God's messenger, came to David to confront him with his sin. When David recognized what he had done, Nathan proclaimed God's word of judgment: "Now therefore," he said, "the sword shall never depart from your house, because you have despised Me and have taken the wife of Uriah the Hittite to be your wife. . . . Behold, I will raise up evil against you from your own household; I will even take your wives before your eyes, and give them to your companion, and he shall lie with your wives in broad daylight" (vv. 10-11). In verse 14 Nathan added that the child born to David and Bathsheba would die. In chapter 13, the Bible reveals the sexual distortions among David's children. Undoubtedly, they were in part encouraged by the example of their father. Then, chapter 15 tells of the rebellion of David's beloved Absalom. Chapter 18 tells of Absalom's death. When you read through the remainder of 2 Samuel, you will see one difficulty after another that came into David's life. It can all be traced back to that lonely night in Jerusalem when David and Bathsheba let sex get out of hand.

There is a message here for us. Uncontrolled sex may bring pleasure for a moment, but it can bring tragedy for a lifetime. It will leave scars that will never be healed.

It will lead to consequences that can never be undone. When you let sex get out of hand, it is going to bring difficulties into your life. You can count on it.

It might be *physical difficulties.* One of the strongest deterrents to sexual promiscuity in the past was fear of detection, fear of infection, and fear of conception. It is commonly thought that with the use of modern methods of protection and medication these are no longer problems. On the contrary, the facts do not support such a conclusion. As recently as 1975, there were an estimated two hundred thousand forced weddings, three hundred thousand girls who had babies outside of marriage, and about one million abortions.[5] In the United States unwanted pregnancies still happen.

Another physical difficulty is disease. Next to the common cold, venereal disease is the most common infectious disease in America. In 1970, there were almost two million cases of gonorrhea. The American Social Health Association estimates that this is only about 11 to 17 percent of the actual cases.[6]

There are also *psychological problems.* The editor of the *American Journal of Psychiatry* says that premarital sex has "greatly increased the number of young people in mental hospitals." [7] As eminent a psychologist as O. Hobart Mowrer declares that anxiety comes not from acts that an individual wants to commit but does not, but from acts that he has committed and wishes he had not.[8] What he means is that the most common cause of modern neuroses is not frustration, but guilt.

You can follow the pied piper of *Playboy* and the new morality if you want to, but you are headed for a rude awakening. You will find that while sex at its best is one of God's greatest gifts, when sex gets out of hand it will bring physical and psychological difficulties in your life.

It Brings a Distorted Understanding

There is more. One cannot read the story of David and Bathsheba without realizing that this is a distortion of what God originally planned for this unique dimension of human life. Likewise, one cannot see what we are doing to sex today without recognizing the same obvious distortion. The worse thing about deviation from God's plan for sex is not that you might get caught or that you might contract a disease. The result most disastrous is that you will develop a distorted picture of what sex is all about. It can be reflected in two ways.

One result will be *domination*. Sex outside of marriage will begin to dominate your relationship. If you let sex get out of hand, it will become the central factor in your relationship and it will prevent you from developing other areas of your relationship. It will, thus, cause your relationship to be out of balance. Sex is to be a part of every marriage relationship. But it is only a part.

The second thing it will do is lead to a kind of *superficiality* in your relationship. Abuse of sex will lead to the point where it becomes simply a casual expression of affection with everyone. But sex was not meant to be a casual addendum to a superficial relationship. Sex was meant to be the climactic culmination of a deep, enduring relationship within the permanent union of a marriage. It was not meant to be an outlet for lust but an outpouring of the deepest kind of human love.

Sex is God's idea and it is good. But when you let sex get out of hand, it will distort your understanding of this gift of God and will change it from love to lust, from a sacred act to a shameful act, from an experience of fulfillment to an experience shrouded with fear, from a part of your relationship to the totality of your relationship. It will lead to distortion in your understanding.

107

It Brings Destruction to the Nation

Nathan told David that because of his sin, "the sword shall never depart from your house" (2 Sam. 12:10). Because of who David was, what affected his house also affected the nation. The result of David's sin was a weakening of the national life, and it began the discouraging descent which eventually led to destruction for Israel.

When we think of the destruction of great nations caused by immorality, we immediately think of the fall of the Roman Empire. But this principle applies on a much broader basis than that. Arnold Toynbee, based on his observation and analysis of nineteen formerly great civilizations, concluded "No nation has ever survived that failed to discipline itself sexually." [9]

This truth is also applicable to our nation. Alexis de Toqueville, the perceptive Frenchman, discovered the true source of America's greatness and genius was in her righteousness. He concluded, "America is great because America is good. If ever America ceases to be good, America will cease to be great."

Conclusion

Maybe you have experienced in your life what David and Bathsheba experienced. Maybe you have let sex get out of hand and have already experienced something of these results I have mentioned.

What can you do? Or more important, what will God do? God will not remove all the consequences. He cannot erase from your life all of the results of your sin. But as David and Bathsheba found forgiveness and renewal of life, so can you. Read Psalm 51 to discover the aftermath of this experience with Bathsheba. Confession which leads to forgiveness is the only answer when sex gets out of hand.

11

Is There Life After Infidelity?

Hosea and Gomer
Hosea 1—3

Sitting in my living room, Bill plodded painfully through the tale of his infidelity. As a sales representative he was away from home most of the week. When he was home, he and his wife (I'll call her Stephanie) were usually at odds with each other. Arguments erupted continuously. The children were out of control. The house was constantly in a mess. There was no warmth in their relationship. It was not a happy home.

That was when Sally, a divorcee, came into the picture. She worked in the branch office in another city where Bill spent two or three days each week. Sally and Bill both were hurting. The commonality of their need drew them together, and an affair developed. The relationship deepened as the weeks passed. Finally, Bill realized that he had to make a choice. He could not continue his dual affection. He carefully considered the pros and cons of each choice and realized that he did not want to leave Stephanie. He did not love Sally. She had simply ministered to a need. He, thus, concluded that his deepest desire was to rekindle the flame of love with his wife. But would Stephanie forgive him? Would she take him back? Could they really get it together again? Was a renewal of their love possible? Those are the questions Bill voiced repeatedly that night in my living room.

Is there life after infidelity? That is a crucial question in our day. Cecil Osborne claims that in 50 percent of today's marriages either the husband or wife commits adultery at least once.[1] That is every other man and every other woman. Other recent reports on the subject suggest similar statistics. Whether or not you accept the accuracy of these reports, the conclusion that infidelity is becoming increasingly more common is inescapable. So ever-present has the problem become that a priest in Los Angeles has begun a new seminar in his church entitled "Affair Prevention" because he says "affairs are epidemic." [2] Perhaps the child was wiser than his teacher thought when he said that after childhood and adolescence, we reach the age of adultery!

Infidelity, however, is no new thing. It was the key factor in a stormy relationship two milleniums ago. This famous couple was Hosea and Gomer, and their story is told in the Old Testament book known by his name. Most commentators on the prophecy of Hosea see in his story an exalted revelation of the love of God for man. What we often forget is that the story of Hosea is, first of all, a marvelous story of the love of a man for a woman who continually betrayed that love.

Hosea 1:2 presents a problem. "Go, take to yourself a wife of harlotry," God told Hosea. Did this mean that Gomer was already a prostitute when Hosea married her? Or did Hosea realize her true character only as he looked back at the experience years later? The latter seems to be the most acceptable interpretation of that vexing verse. Why? For one thing, the marriage of Hosea and Gomer was supposed to be an analogy of God's relationship with Israel. Israel, however, was pure at the beginning. Only later did she play the harlot. Thus, the latter interpretation is necessary for the symbolism of the book to correspond to the reality of Israel's history. In addition, for Hosea to have married a harlot would have exposed him to the contempt of his contemporaries. His mission was to

110

condemn the conduct of his countrymen. To marry a known harlot would have seemed to condone their conduct.

So this is the picture. Hosea married a woman from whom he expected total commitment. Instead, she became involved in sexual relationships with other men. Not just once, but continually! Infidelity and how to deal with it is the theme that weaves its way through this Old Testament prophecy.

That is where the story touches us today. The week I wrote this chapter I had three church members call for help in dealing with the problem of infidelity. It is Bill and Stephanie's story all over again. Charlie Shedd concluded that the temptation to infidelity is not an isolated matter, but "standard equipment on some of the best models." [3] Let's take a look at the problem.

The Reasons for Infidelity

In a recent Woman Poll, 70 percent of the women questioned about infidelity stated that if their husband were having an affair the first thing they would want to know was, "Why?" [4] Why are husbands and wives unfaithful?

In the story of Hosea and Gomer, we are given few hints as to the motivation for Gomer's unfaithfulness. To the increasing number of those involved in adultery who come to me for counseling, I always direct this question: "How did it happen?" The answers usually fall into one of four categories.

Closeness is the most common answer. The close associations with a person at work often present overwhelming temptations.

Picture a typical rising executive. His work dominates the hours of his day. Who is it that communicates with him most fully about his work? His secretary. Or maybe a woman associate. She is well-groomed, well-dressed, and well-informed. She shares his goals and is his co-worker in attaining those goals. Emotional moments are unavoidably shared with her, and the man spends the best hours of his day with her. The wife, who as a house-wife bids him farewell in the morning in her dirty robe and with her hair uncombed and welcomes him home in the evening with her complaints about the children or the plumbing, gradually becomes less appealing. Or if she works, her career often moves her in a direction out of pace with his. Add to that the natural maternal, nurturing impulse in most women which often surfaces in a consoling secretary, and you have set the context for a possible affair. It is not planned, nor is it necessarily desired. It just happens.

Problems in the husband's or wife's relationship also contribute to affairs. One counselee said to me, "My husband told me if he didn't get sex at home, he would get it somewhere!" Although most people are not so blunt about it, the truth nevertheless stands. Sexual dissatisfaction at home may lead to attempts for satisfaction elsewhere.

Or, at times, the problems may be in other areas of marriage. Communication problems in the marriage relationship often provide excuses for communication of the ultimate type, sexual communication, outside of marriage. Preoccupation with children or with other interests can open the door for an affair. Depression over a business failure can also be a factor. More often than not, infidelity is the result of a marriage breakdown rather than the cause of it. Infidelity is a sign of some deep, underlying deficiency in the relationship.

"The Playboy philosophy" is also a primary factor in the apparent increasing participation in infidelity. This is what John Drakeford calls "The Great Sex Swindle." [5]

The Playboy philosophy emanates from two focuses. One is a biological theory of sex. Like hunger, the sexual drive is merely a biological urge. According to this theory, to satisfy the sexual urge when and where you need to is the only natural thing to do. The other key is an anti-religious bias. Morality is the tool religion uses to control people. The Playboy philosophy discards what it considers to be outdated morality in favor of the pleasure principle. Right is what feels good. This idea, of course, is rooted in the Freudian conclusion that anxiety comes from the acts which an individual wants to do but dares not do. Repression is man's basic personality problem, according to Freud, and the solution is freedom to fulfill the instinctual demands.

It is frightening how that philosophy has pervaded our society. A woman was in my office recently. Her husband had concluded the confession of his continuous affairs to her with this remark, "It's just the natural thing to do. Everybody is doing it." The constant bombardment of our minds by this philosophy of permissiveness creates a spark which often erupts into a flame when the opportunity presents itself. The temporarily titillating thrill promised by a clandestine rendezvous has a strong appeal.

Another important ingredient leading to infidelity is *personal difficulties*. Let's face it, immaturity and selfishness are primal causes of unfaithfulness. Arthur Adams, dean of Princeton Theological Seminary, rightly declared, "adultery is the sacrament of selfishness." [6]

At any age, personal problems can wreck havoc. The personal problems are intensified, however, during the middle years. Menopause in women and its counterpart in men often erupt into insecurity, depression, and a need for a reaffirmation. This entrance into the "Deadline Decade," Gail Sheehy describes like this: "The loss of youth, the faltering of physical powers we have always taken for granted, the fading purpose of stereotyped roles by which we have thus far identified ourselves—any or all of these shocks can give this passage the character of crisis." [7]

Infidelity often happens in this crisis time as men try to prove their virility and women their desirability. The ego needs to be inflated. In such cases, sex is not so much the motive for self-assertion as it is the method of self-assertion. Ego is the motive.

The only clue to the behavior of Gomer is in Hosea 3:3. After he bought her back, Hosea kept Gomer in seclusion. He prevented her from being exposed to other men. The implication is that she had a personality problem that made her unusually susceptible to infidelity. Any of the other three suggestions above could also have come into play.

The Reaction to Infidelity

The young lady broke into tears as she sat down in my office. "My husband is having an affair," she blurted out, "and I don't know what to do. I just can't take him back. But I can't stand to think about losing him." That's the dilemma! After infidelity, what can you do? What reaction can you make? You have several choices.

One option is *retaliation*. "If he can do it, so can I." "I'll show him." "I'll teach her to hurt me." Those responses are all expressions of the desire to retaliate. Webster defines retaliation as "punishment in kind," "to pay back injury for injury."

A recent Women Poll indicated that this would be the response of only about 1 percent of the women questioned.[8] Linda Wolf, in an article in *Ladies Home Journal,* concurred that this approach is not a healthy one because she said "in the end both partners are so secretive and out of touch with one another that their marriage comes apart out of sheer disuse." [9] Seeking revenge might bring a temporary sense of satisfaction, but in the end nobody wins.

A second response is *resignation*. This is the conclusion that infidelity has created an irreparable rift in the relationship. Divorce is thus the only out. With the increased acceptability of divorce, it has become the primary coping mechanism for infidelity. One counselee told me, "I could never trust him again." Another stated that she simply could not erase from her mind the picture of her husband and his lover in bed together. The viability of this option becomes more appealing when, as is so often the case, infidelity is discovered to have been a long-established pattern rather than a one-time clandestine happening.

Many couples opt for a third alternative that could be called *accommodation*. That is, the hurt party simply ignores the infidelity. Although one lady declared that if her husband had a fling, "the only thing I wouldn't do is ignore it," the fact is that many do.[10] How could a person ignore infidelity? It could be for psychological reasons. The fear of being alone in some cases is greater than the hurt of infidelity. Economy can also be a factor. A counselee recently told me that she would have already divorced her husband, who had been involved with another woman, except for the financial stability he provided. Sometimes it is because of the children. "I told him I would stay with him until the children get out of school," is a common response. Or, it could be religious reasons. There are some for whom divorce is simply not an option. Better to continue the facade of marriage than to invite the judgment of God because of a divorce. That this response is often made to infidelity is evident. It is just as evident that a relationship which survives an affair by the alternative of accommodation will probably be neither healthy nor mutually rewarding.

A fourth possibility is *continuation.* This is accommodation with your eyes open. This is to face the problem of infidelity with the question, "What can we make out of our relationship now? How can we learn? What does this experience tell us about the deficiencies in our relationship?" Whether or not this option is possible will be dealt with in the last section.

What did Hosea do? Obviously he did not retaliate. There is no suggestion in Scripture of this. Nor did he take the pathway of resignation. Some suggest that Hosea divorced Gomer. This, however, is not said in the text. It seems that instead of Hosea kicking Gomer out, she chose to go live with her latest paramour. Neither did Hosea simply ignore the problem. The fact that he named his child, Lo-ammi (none of mine), implies that he knew the truth about her. Also, his action in Hosea 3:3 shows that he took definite steps to correct the problem. The fourth alternative was definitely the one Hosea chose. But that leads to a further consideration.

The Recovery from Infidelity

Can there be life after infidelity? I have counseled with many couples whose marriage was shaken by the problem of infidelity. Whether or not they were able to rebuild their relationship depended on several factors.

The basic ingredient is *forgiveness.* For a million and one hurts and disappointments forgiveness is the salve that brings healing. Likewise, for the psychic injury of infidelity forgiveness is the only cure.

Forgiveness, of course, assumes repentance. One of the biggest lies propagated on the American public came from the popular movie *Love Story.* For millions of impressionable young people who viewed the film "Love means never having to say you are sorry." That's a lie. Love means being able to say, "I'm sorry."

In a recent discussion a man told me of his wife's infidelity. I asked him if he could have ever forgiven her. He said, "Yes, if she would have showed me that she really wanted to make a go of it." That is, if she would have repented and reflected a desire to make a change. "I'm sorry" and "I forgive" will be at the heart of any marriage that is resurrected from the graveyard of infidelity.

Forgive and forget. It's harder to do the latter sometimes than the former. But an important step which will lead to healing in a broken relationship is *forgetfulness.*

To forget means to put out of your mind and to remove from your conversation. It means to refuse to bring up the subject. Not when you are mad. Not when your husband or wife hurts you. Not when you want to manipulate your mate into doing what you want. Never! Infidelity causes a deep gash in a marriage, but the passing of time can bring healing to the wound. A constant reminder of the incident, however is like picking the scab on a physical wound. It will prevent proper healing.

When the memory of infidelity comes up, replace it with positive thoughts. Counter the acts of unfaithfulness with a list of the evidences of faith which your mate has given.

The next step is *fortitude.* Fortitude means courage. Or persistence. Or determination. I am happy to report that Bill and Stephanie, with whose story I began this chapter, did stay together. I shared with them quite intimately during the reconstruction of their marriage. From all appearances their marriage is stronger than it was before. Why? Because they determined that they were going to make it happen, and they have worked at it. They spend time together. He is careful not to do anything which would cause her to question her trust in him. They openly express their concern and affection. They work at it. And gradually the trust is returning and the wound is healing.

I counseled with one couple over a year. On their first visit, everything about their situation pointed to a dissolution of their marriage. Nearly three years later they are still together. I asked the wife how she felt. She said, "The pain is still there. But we're doing better." That's fortitude.

I like to believe that Hosea and Gomer made it, too. We don't know for sure. But I believe they did. The reason I believe that is the courageous love which Hosea expressed in chapter 3 of his book. This kind of love which continues (v. 1), redeems (v. 2) and courageously deals with the problem (v. 3) will eventually be a love which triumphs (vv. 4-5).

Conclusion

Can there be life after infidelity? Yes, in some cases. Often, however, the hurt is too deep or the desire too shallow. Sometimes there are too many painful reminders lingering around. But some couples like Hosea and Gomer, or like Bill and Stephanie, can discover that perfect blend of forgivenenss, forgetfulness, and fortitude to make it happen.

12
On Target

Aquila and Priscilla
Acts 18:1-3

One thing about the Bible—it does not cover up the shortcomings of its characters. This honesty of the Bible has been clearly evident in our study of these biblical couples. These couples were not perfect by any means. In fact, they were much like couples today. They knew what it was like to see a good beginning turn sour, to experience the trauma of middlescence, to disagree over in-laws, to have difficulty handling money and sex, to face the insult of infidelity and the enigma of indifference. They were plagued with problems and in many ways fell short of God's ideal for marriage.

After some of the problem marriages we have discussed, it is like a breath of fresh air to see a couple that displays in their marriage a dedication to the divine design, a couple that is "on target" as far as God's purpose for the home is concerned. We see such a couple in Priscilla and Aquila. These young tentmakers, companions of Paul, co-workers in his ministry, courageous followers of Christ, are mentioned six times in the New Testament.

Acts 18:1-3 introduces Aquila and Priscilla as tentmakers who were expelled from Rome because Aquila was a Jewess. They went with Paul from Corinth to Ephesus where they remained for awhile as teachers. It was here that they took Apollos aside and tutored him in the faith (Acts 18:18,26). They are mentioned again in Paul's epilogue in First Corinthians. Here Paul refers to the church in their house (1 Cor. 16:19). We find quite a testimony to Aquila and Priscilla in Romans 16:3-4 where Paul rejoices over their commitment ("my helpers in Christ Jesus," KJV), their courage ("for my life laid down their own necks," KJV), and their widespread influence ("unto whom not only I give thanks, but also all the churches of the Gentiles," KJV). Again they are given greeting in 2 Timothy 4:19.

In these brief references we have a beautiful portrait of a couple who really had it together. At three points they were on target.

They Experienced Togetherness

The first thing we see is that Priscilla and Aquila experienced a true sense of togetherness. An examination of the Scripture references to them will show that they are always mentioned together. One is never mentioned without the other. This implies a togetherness—an intimacy—which made them truly one.

That's what God wants for every marriage. Genesis 2:18 says that the reason God created Eve for Adam was that they may be companions with each other, experiencing a real sense of oneness. Genesis 2:24 says, "For this cause a man shall leave his father and his mother, and shall cleave to his wife; and they shall become one flesh."

The purpose of marriage is that two individuals may be literally "glued together" in a one-flesh kind of relationship that is characterized by intimacy and togetherness and oneness. With no companionship, with no togetherness, with no intimacy, marriage has no meaning.

The tragedy of many marriages today is that we do not experience this togetherness. Why? In part, it is because we do not understand what togetherness is. Togetherness does not mean simple propinquity—that is, just being geographically near each other. There are couples who are together a great deal who do not really experience togetherness. Nor is togetherness to be found only in the sexual relationship, although that is a vital part of it. Rather, as Howard and Charlotte Clinebell point out, togetherness is a multifaceted thing that involves every dimension of our lives. There is emotional intimacy (the depth sharing of significant feelings), intellectual intimacy (the sharing in the world of ideas), aesthetic intimacy (the depth sharing of experiences of beauty), creative intimacy (the sharing of acts of creativity), recreational intimacy (sharing activities and fun times), work intimacy (sharing in common tasks), crisis intimacy (standing together against the buffeting of life), spiritual intimacy (the sharing of ultimate concerns), and sexual intimacy.[1] True togetherness comes as we experience intimacy in each of these areas.

We do not have the fully detailed story on Priscilla and Aquila but we can assume their intimacy was one which was based on shared activities in every area of their lives. They were one spiritually. That much is evident. They also knew the joy of work intimacy. Their relationship to Apollos implies intellectual intimacy. The challenge of being a Christian in that day provided the opportunity for crisis intimacy. The intimacy of Aquila and Priscilla involved every facet of their lives. Togetherness like that which Priscilla and Aquila experienced—that's what marriage is all about.

How can we have it in our marriage?

1. To desire it is the first step. Come to the point where you are dissatisfied with anything less than real oneness, where you are tired of just existing in marriage. Take an intimacy inventory of your marriage. That is, carefully evaluate your marriage in each of the dimensions of intimacy discussed above. See the areas where you do not

have the desired togetherness and determine to do something about it. Desire it.

2. Honesty is also required. Be willing to open your deepest self to each other. Intimacy comes as you gradually lower the masks and barriers which protect your inner self and allow your soul to touch the soul of your mate.

3. For intimacy to be experienced there must also be genuine concern, and it must be expressed. In word and in deed, on a daily basis, express your love to your mate. In the context of loving concern the barriers can be lowered and intimacy can be developed.

4. A climate of trust in your marriage is necessary as well. Leave no questions or doubts about your fidelity and complete commitment to each other. It is only as you come to the point where you completely trust each other that you will open your souls to each other.

5. Then spend time with each other. Several years ago a twister swept through the farmlands of Kansas and touched down right by a farmhouse. The force of the wind lifted the roof off and set it down about fifty feet from the house. It also lifted up the bed on which the husband and wife were asleep and set it down in the front yard. Immediately the wife began to cry. As the husband tried to comfort her he whispered, "Don't cry, honey. Everything's all right. Don't be afraid." "I'm not afraid," she said, "I'm crying because I am happy. This is the first time in five years we've been out of the house together!"

Priscilla and Aquila experienced togetherness.

They Were Able to Adjust

A second thing we see about Priscilla and Aquila is that they were able to adjust. Like every couple they faced changes and conflicts and crises with which they had to deal.

In Acts 18:2, we see that they were forced to leave Italy. In A.D. 52 Claudius passed a decree banning all Jews from the imperial city of Rome. If, as tradition tells us, Priscilla was a member of a blueblooded family of Rome, her marriage to a Jew and then their forced expulsion from her beloved home city was a crisis of monumental magnitude.

Another challenge to their marriage was their constant moves. They keep showing up in the Scriptures references in different places. They were constantly on the move, meeting new people, living in new cities, facing new situations.

We also notice that no children are mentioned which may imply that they did not have any. If true, what a trauma this was. In a day and time when children were "an inheritance from the Lord," and "blessed is the man whose quiver is full of them" this would have been a supreme setback. Even today nothing is quite so traumatic as a couple which wants to have a child but cannot.

There is no marriage which does not face similar crises. In fact, most couples are confronted by almost daily conflict within their relationship. An old German proverb says, "Every seven years marriage has a crisis." Most of us admit that they come much more frequently than that.

How can we deal with this conflict? How can we adjust to the continuing crises of marriage, the daily dilemmas that come our way?

1. *Communication.*—Before these resentments build up within, we must talk them out. Many marriages have gone on the rocks simply because people have refused to acknowledge their problems and failed to communicate

about them. When you have a problem one of you has to have the courage to say, "Let's talk" and both have to be willing to do it. Communication means to express what you really feel, to establish the positions. There will be no adjustment without that.

2. *Assimilation.*—Once the conflict is brought out into the open and the communication begins and the positions are defined, it is sometimes possible for one person to accept the view of the other and assimilate that into his own life. That is, you see that the other person is right or at least partly right, so you move over to his/her position. If so, the problem is solved.

3. *Accommodation.*—Sometimes the two positions still remain, so compromise has to take place. In the give and take of accommodation many conflicts can be satisfactorily resolved.

4. *Toleration.*—There are times when a compromise is not possible so the couple agrees to disagree. Each partner holds to his own viewpoint and tolerates it. Each knows where the other person stands and each respects the other person's position.

5. *Cancellation.*—Once the conflict has been discussed and settled, whether by assimilation, accommodation, or toleration, put it behind you. Bury it. Cancel it out of your mind. I heard of one wife who kept bringing up a conflict after they had agreed to forget it because she wanted him to remember that she had forgotten it! Once a problem has been settled, it needs to be forgotten.

Let me give an example of how this procedure works out. Suppose there is a problem over the schedule for Saturday. Every Saturday the husband goes to play golf. It is mid-afternoon before he gets in. For the wife this makes Saturday just like every other day. No relief from the children, no companionship with the husband. The hostility gradually builds. One day the husband notices something is bothering his wife so he asks her what is on her mind. (Remember, we are using our imagination!) So she tells him. She feels like Saturday should be a family day. She needs him and the children do, too. He counters with his need for relaxation after the rigors of a week at work. That's communication. The positions are established. If the wife is convinced by the husband's presentation or if the husband is convicted by his family's need, one may give in. The husband says, "You're right, honey. I won't play golf on Saturday anymore." That's assimilation. Suppose neither gives in. A compromise is needed. They agree that the morning belongs to the husband for golf. He'll only play nine holes so he can be home by noon. The afternoon belongs to them. They plan the agenda. That's accommodation. To maintain the original course with neither budging is toleration. Cancellation is not possible in this case. Only if the conflict is handled by step two or three can the matter be put out of mind.

Marriages that are on target like Priscilla and Aquila's are not marriages without conflicts to confront, but those that are able to face these conflicts and work through them, couples who are able to adjust.

They Put God at the Center

Another important element in the relationship of Priscilla and Aquila is that they put God at the center of their home. In chapter 1 we saw that this was one of the ways Adam and Eve went wrong. Priscilla and Aquila did not repeat that mistake. They put God first.

This is evident as we reflect on the Scripture references to them. Acts 18:18 shows them going out as missionaries. In Acts 18:26 they are involved in Christian teaching. First Corinthians 16:19 mentions Priscilla and Aquila and the church that is in their home. In Romans 16:3, Paul singles them out as "My fellow workers in Christ

Jesus." Why? Not because they were great preachers like Peter, or great writers like Matthew, or great thinkers like John, or great missionaries like Barnabas, or great organizers like Titus, but because they were a husband and wife who dared to put God first in their home.

E. Stanley Jones spent many years of his life in India, where in his ashrams he confronted people with the claims of Christ. He told of one lady who came to the ashram one day. She and her husband were in constant conflict. She refused to get up and fix his breakfast. He adamantly felt she should; and they were constantly at each other's throat. In the experience with Christians in that fellowship gathering this lady made her surrender to Christ and was converted.

As she left she asked, "Mr. Jones, what shall I do when I get home?" She was told to go home and tell her husband she was the cause of all their problems. She said, "I can't do that. I believe he is the cause of our problems and he says I am." Jones told her, "Go pray about it." After praying she decided to give it a try.

The next morning she got up and fixed her husband's breakfast—which she had not done in years. Her husband was shocked and knew something was different. Rather suspiciously he said, "Well, Miss High and Mighty, what did you learn at the ashram?" She said, "I learned I am the cause of all our problems." She got up from her chair, came around the table and knelt by her husband, folded her hands and said, "Please forgive me, for I am the cause of all our troubles." She said that he almost turned the table over getting down on his knees beside her. He blurted out, "No, you're not the cause of our problems. I am." And in that moment of self-confession, they met God, and came together. Each surrendered to God, and then they surrendered to each other, and then they were set free! [2]

That needs to happen in many homes today. The greatest source of heartache and tension in many marriages is the simple fact that one or both of the partners is out of fellowship with God. The husband and wife never read the Bible together. They never pray together. They don't go to church together. God is not at the center of their home.

I want to tell you something. Even if you share the closest intimacy possible in your marriage, if God is not at the center of your home then your marriage is not on target. Even if you are able to adjust to every conflict that comes your way, if God is not at the center of your home, then your marriage is not on target. A marriage that is on target begins when each partner puts God in charge of his life.

Conclusion

John Howard Payne, lonely and homesick, shivered on the streets of a city on the other side of the world. As he inched down the street, he saw a door open for just a minute. A shaft of light fell across the snow and a spark of life was seen within. He saw a husband go in the door and saw his wife welcome him in a warm embrace. As he went back to his room, inspired by that brief scene of a loving embrace, he penned the immortal words:

> Mid pleasures and palaces
>   though we may roam,
> Be it ever so humble,
>   there's no place like home.[3]

That song beautifully describes the home of Priscilla and Aquila. If you will develop a real experience of intimacy, adjust to your conflicts in a healthy way, and put God at the center of your home, then your marriage can be on target, too.

Notes

Preface
1. James A. Peterson, *Married Love in the Middle Years* (New York: Association Press, 1968), p. 20.

Chapter 1
1. Joyce Brothers, "Make Your Marriage a Love Affair," *Reader's Digest* (March, 1973), p. 79.
2. Tim Le Haye, *How to Be Happy Though Married* (Wheaton: Tyndale House Publications, 1968), p. 117.
3. Cecil Osborne, *The Art of Understanding Your Mate* (Grand Rapids: Zondervan Publishing House, 1970), p. 88.
4. Robert W. Burns, *The Art of Staying Happily Married* (Englewood Cliffs, N.J.: Prentice-Hall, Inc., 1963), p. 110.

Chapter 2
1. Bernard Harnik, *Risk and Chance in Marriage* (Waco: Word Books, 1972), p. 107.
2. Peterson, p. 20.
3. Osborne, p. 70.
4. Peterson, p. 38.
5. Gail Sheehy, *Passages* (New York: E. P. Dutton & Co., Inc., 1974), p. 37.
6. Harnik, pp. 18-19.
7. John Henry C. Newman, *The Development of Christian Doctrine* (New York: Longmans, Green & Co., 1949), p. 38.
8. Peterson, p. 56.

Chapter 3
1. Harnik, p. 26.
2. David and Vera Mace, *We Can Have Better Marriages* (Nashville: Abingdon Press, 1974), p. 65.
3. See Cleveland McDonald, *Creating a Successful Christian Marriage* (Grand Rapids: Baker Book House, 1975), pp. 277-78 for an excellent discussion of intermarriage.
4. Albert I. Gordon, *Intermarriage, Interfaith, Interracial, Interethnic* (Boston: Beacon Press, 1964), p. 372.

5. Harnik, p. 44.

6. E. E. LeMasters, *Modern Courtship and Marriage* (New York: The Macmillan Company, 1957), p. 488.

7. Paul Tournier, *To Understand Each Other* (Richmond, Va.: John Knox Press, 1967), p. 38.

8. Mace, *Better Marriages,* p. 61.

9. Elton and Pauline Trueblood, *The Recovery of Family Life* (New York: Harper & Row, 1953), p. 57.

Chapter 4

1. Harnik, p. 125.

2. Eric Berne, *Games People Play* (New York: Grove Press, Inc., 1964), pp. 92-110.

3. Burns, p. 194.

4. Harnik, p. 90.

5. Charlie W. Shedd, *Letters to Karen* (Nashville: Abingdon Press, 1965), p. 154.

Chapter 5

1. Larry and Nordis Christenson, *The Christian Couple* (Minneapolis, Minn.: Bethany Fellowship, Inc., 1977), p. 16.

2. *Quote,* Vol. 72., p. 573.

3. Charlotte H. and Howard J., Jr. Clinebell, *The Intimate Marriage* (New York: Harper & Row, 1970), p. 67.

4. Dorothy W. Baruch, *How to Live with Your Teenager* (New York: McGraw-Hill, 1953), p. 23.

5. The *Good News Bible* translates the verse to say that Othniel persuaded Achsah to go ask Caleb for the land. The Hebrew text, however, is clear that it is Achsah who tried to persuade Othniel. Upon failing to do that, she went to Caleb herself. All the major translations project this idea—NASB, RSV, and KJV.

6. Burns, p. 165.

7. Robert O. Blood and Donald M. Wolfe, *Husbands and Wives* (New York: The Free Press of Glencoe, 1960), p. 245.

8. MacDonald, p. 223.

9. Burns, p. 160.

10. John Bisagno, *Love Is Something You Do* (New York: Harper & Row, 1975), p. 98.

11. Washington Gladden, "Knowing How to Be Rich" in *Twenty Centuries of Great Preaching,* Vol. VI, edited by Clyde

E. Fant, Jr. and William M. Pinson, Jr. (Waco: Word Books, 1971), p. 204.

Chapter 6

1. John Drakeford, *Do You Hear Me, Honey?* (New York: Harper & Row, 1976), p. 6.

2. Charlie Shedd, *Talk to Me* (Garden City, N.Y.: Doubleday and Co., Inc., 1975), p. 13.

3. Tournier, p. 25.

4. From *The Real Self* (A series of cassette tapes published and copyrighted by Human Development Institutes, Chicago, 1973).

5. Mace, *Better Marriages,* p. 87.

6. Tournier, p. 19.

7. Reuel L. Howe, *Herein Is Love* (Valley Forge, Pa.: The Judson Press, 1961), p. 100.

8. Shedd, *Talk to Me,* p. 24.

9. John Drakeford, *How to Manipulate Your Mate,* (New York: Thomas Nelson, Inc., 1974), pp. 97-98.

10. Philip Yancey, *After the Wedding* (Waco: Word Books, 1976), pp. 110-11.

11. Landrum P. Leavell, *Sermons for Celebrating* (Nashville: Broadman Press, 1978), p. 93.

Chapter 7

1. Leonard Benson, *The Family Bond: Marriage, Love, and Sex* (New York: Random House, 1971), p. 312.

2. Norval D. Glenn and Charles N. Weaver, "The Marital Happiness of Remarried Divorce Persons" in *The Journal of Marriage and the Family* (May, 1977), p. 335.

3. Jesse Bernard, *Remarriage* (New York: The Dryden Press, 1956), p. 15.

4. Walter C. McKain, "A New Look at Older Marriages," in *The Family Coordinator* (January, 1972), pp. 14-16.

5. Janet Harbison Penfield, "Second Time Around" in *Christian Herald* (August, 1975), p. 30.

6. Ralph W. Neighbour, Jr. and Cal Thomas, *Target* Group Evangelism (Nashville: Broadman Press, 1975), pp. 107-10.

7. Granger E. Westberg, *Good Grief* (Philadelphia: Fortress Press, 1962). The entire book is a development of these ten stages.

8. Herbert Lockyer, *The Women of the Bible* (Grand Rapids: Zondervan Publishing House, 1967), p. 145.

9. Burns, p. 120.

Chapter 8

1. Judson T. and Mary G. Landis, *Building a Successful Marriage* (Englewood Cliffs, N.J.: Prentice Hall, 1953), pp. 302-303.

2. Evelyn Duvall and Reuben Hill, *Being Married* (New York: Association Press, 1960), p. 211.

3. Evelyn Duvall, *In-Laws: Pro and Con* (New York: Association Press, 1954), p. 191.

4. John Drakeford, *Marriage: Duet or Discord* (Grand Rapids: Zondervan Publishing House, 1965), p. 75.

5. *Pro and Con,* p. 9.

6. Kay K. Arvin, *1 + 1 = 1* (Nashville: Broadman Press, 1969), p. 72.

7. *Pro and Con,* p. 163.

8. David Knox, *Marriage Happiness: A Behavioral Approach to Counseling* (Champaign, Ill.: Research Press Co., 1971), p. 64.

9. *Pro and Con,* p. 325.

Chapter 9

1. Susan Nelson, "How Battered Women Can Get Help," *Reader's Digest* (May, 1977), p. 21.

2. *Quote,* Vol. 74, p. 145.

3. Drakeford, *Do You Hear Me, Honey?* p. 104.

4. Elton Trueblood, *A Place to Stand* (New York: Harper and Row, 1969), p. 28.

5. Osborne, p. 221.

6. John Claypool, "The Choice Is Always Ours," preached at Northminister Baptist Church, Jackson, Mississippi.

7. Osborne, p. 24.

Chapter 10

1. See John Drakeford, *Marriage: Duet or Discord,* p. 48.

2. Joyce Landorf, *Tough and Tender* (Old Tappan: Fleming H. Revell, 1975), p. 127.

3. Letha Scanzoni, *Why Wait?* (Grand Rapids: Baker Book House, 1975), p. 93.

131

4. David Mace, *Whom God Hath Joined* (Philadelphia: The Westminster Press, 1973), p. 40.

5. A. Dudley Dennison, *Give It to Me Straight, Doctor* (Grand Rapids: Zondervan, 1972), p. 28.

6. *Ibid.,* p. 29.

7. *Ibid.*

8. John Drakeford, *The Great Sex Swindle* (Nashville: Broadman Press, 1966), p. 50.

9. Nelson Price, *Shadows We Run From* (Nashville: Broadman Press, 1975), p. 96.

Chapter 11

1. Osborne, p. 121.

2. *Dallas Morning News,* January 2, 1978.

3. Charlie W. Shedd, *Letters to Philip: On How to Treat a Woman* (Garden City: Doubleday and Co., Inc., 1968), p. 120.

4. *Dallas Morning News,* August 23, 1977, p. 3c.

5. Drakeford, *The Great Sex Swindle.*

6. Arthur M. Adams, "The Sacrament of Selfishness" in *The Princeton Seminary Bulletin* (Winter, 1976), p. 74.

7. Sheehy, p. 35.

8. *Dallas Morning News,* August 23, 1977, p. 3c.

9. Linda Wolfe, "The Unfaithful Husband," *The Ladies Home Journal* (August, 1977), p. 134.

10. *Dallas Morning News,* August 23, 1977, p. 3c.

Chapter 12

1. Clinebell, pp. 28-31.

2. E. Stanley Jones, *Victory Through Surrender* (Nashville: Abingdon Press, 1966), p. 127.

3. W. Herschell Ford, *Heaven, Hell, and Judgment* (Grand Rapids: Zondervan Publishing House, 1965), pp. 39-40.